"The business and culture surrounding video games have not stopped evolving, and neither has researchers' understanding of the new issues and debates that come with those changes. The experts in this book lay them all out in clear, well-supported summaries that leave the reader deeply informed."

Jamie Madigan, *Author of The Engagement Game: Why Your Workplace Culture Should Look More Like a Video Game*

THE VIDEO GAME DEBATE 2

This student-friendly book provides an accessible overview of the primary debates about the effects of video games. It expands on the original *The Video Game Debate* to address the new technologies that have emerged within the field of game studies over the last few years.

Debates about the negative effects of video game play have been evident since their introduction in the 1970s, but the advent of online and mobile gaming has revived these concerns, reinvigorating old debates and generating brand new ones. *The Video Game Debate 2* draws from the latest research findings from the top scholars of digital games research to address these concerns. The book explores key developments such as virtual and augmented reality, the use of micro-transactions, the integration of loot boxes, and the growth of mobile gaming and games for change (serious games). Furthermore, several new chapters explore contemporary debates around e-sports, gamification, sex and gender discrimination in games, and the use of games in therapy.

This book offers students and scholars of games studies and digital media, as well as policymakers, the essential information they need to participate in the debate.

Rachel Kowert is the Research Director of *Take This*, a nonprofit organization that provides mental health information and resources to gaming communities and the gaming industry. She has been studying games and gamers for more than 10 years, with a specific focus on the social impact of digital game play. She has published numerous research articles and books on the topic, including *A Parent's Guide to Video Games* (2016), which won an INDIES award in science. For more information on Rachel and her research, please visit rkowert.com.

Thorsten Quandt is Professor of Online Communication at the University of Münster and a distinguished scientist with extensive experience in digital games research, both nationally and internationally. He is the founding chair of the ECREA section on Digital Games Research, and the co-editor of essential books in game studies, including *Multiplayer* (2013), *The Video Game Debate* (2016), and *New Perspectives on the Social Aspects of Digital Gaming* (2017).

Routledge Debates in Digital Media Studies

Series editors: Rachel Kowert and Thorsten Quandt

The Routledge Debates in Digital Media Studies series provides critical examinations of the active debates that surround the uses and effects of new media and technologies within society. Consisting of essays written by leading scholars and experts, each volume tackles a growing area of inquiry and debate in the field and provides readers with an in-depth and accessible overview of the topic in question.

The Video Game Debate 2
Revisiting the Physical, Social, and Psychological Effects of Video Games
Edited by Rachel Kowert and Thorsten Quandt

For more information about this series, please visit: https://www.routledge.com/Routledge-Debates-in-Digital-Media-Studies/book-series/RDDMS

THE VIDEO GAME DEBATE 2

Revisiting the Physical, Social, and Psychological Effects of Video Games

Edited by Rachel Kowert and Thorsten Quandt

Routledge
Taylor & Francis Group

NEW YORK AND LONDON

First published 2021
by Routledge
52 Vanderbilt Avenue, New York, NY 10017

and by Routledge
2 Park Square, Milton Park, Abingdon, Oxon, OX14 4RN

Routledge is an imprint of the Taylor & Francis Group, an informa business

© 2021 Taylor & Francis

Library of Congress Cataloging-in-Publication Data
A catalog record for this title has been requested.

ISBN: 978-0-367-36872-2 (hbk)
ISBN: 978-0-367-36694-0 (pbk)
ISBN: 978-0-429-35181-5 (ebk)

Typeset in Bembo
by MPS Limited, Dehradun

CONTENTS

Illustrations

Figure

Tables

CONTRIBUTORS

Kati Alha, MSc, is a researcher and a university lecturer, teaching game studies at Tampere University, Finland. She has been a part of Tampere University Game Research Lab since 2009 and studied games from multiple perspectives, with the fields of expertise in free-to-play games, location-based games, playability, and player experiences. Alha is currently finalizing her dissertation focusing on game experiences provided by free-to-play games.

Tom Thomas H. Apperley, PhD, is a Senior Research Fellow (Yliopistotutkija) at the Centre of Excellence in Game Culture Studies. He conducts research on digital games and playful technologies with an emphasis on their impact and influence on culture, particularly areas such as social policy, pedagogy, and social inclusion. His open-access print-on-demand book *Gaming Rhythms: Play and Counterplay from the Situated to the Global*, was published by The Institute of Network Cultures in 2010.

Anthony Bean, PhD, is a licensed psychologist, video game researcher, and executive director at The Telos Project, a nonprofit mental health clinic in Fort Worth, Texas. He specializes in the therapeutic implications of video games, gaming, and geek therapy and works with children, adolescents, and adults on character identification as a therapeutic technique. He is the founder of Geek Therapy Training and Certified Geek Therapist Training, which can be found at geektherapytraining.com/.

Ashley M.L. Brown, PhD, is an assistant professor at Entertainment Arts and Engineering, The University of Utah, where she teaches games user research and runs a user testing lab. She has been Twitch streaming a variety of games and academic and non-academic content since 2018 at her channel twitch.tv/professor_ashley. The bulk of her current research interests concern how live streaming and virtual classrooms impact pedagogy in higher education.

Kishonna L. Gray, PhD, is an assistant professor in Communication and Gender and Women's Studies at the University of Illinois at Chicago and is a Faculty Associate at the Berkman-Klein Centre for Internet & Society at Harvard University. Her work intersects identity and digital media with a focus on video games and gaming culture. Her book *Race, Gender, & Deviance in Xbox Live* examines the reality of women and people of color in one of the largest gaming communities. Her new book *Intersectional Tech: Black Users in Digital Gaming* is forthcoming in 2020 from LSU Press. She is the co-editor of two recent collections on gaming: *Woke Gaming: Digital Challenges to Oppression and Social Injustice* (with David Leonard) from University of Washington Press and *Women in Games, Feminism in Play* (with Gerald Voorhees and Emma Vossen) from Palgrave. Her other recent work is featured in the journals *Frontiers: A Journal of Women's Studies, Gender, Technology and Development, Journal of Lesbian Studies,* and *Velvet Light Trap.*

Mark D. Griffiths, PhD, is a Chartered Psychologist and Distinguished Professor of Behavioural Addiction at the Nottingham Trent University, and Director of the International Gaming Research Unit. He has spent 33 years in the field and is internationally known for his work into gambling, gaming, and behavioral addictions. He has published over 990 refereed research papers, five books, 150+ book chapters, and over 1,500 other articles. He has won 22 national and international awards for his work including the John Rosecrance Prize (1994), CELEJ Prize (1998), Joseph Lister Prize (2004), and the US National Council on Problem Gambling Lifetime Research Award (2013). He also does a lot of freelance journalism and has appeared on over 3,500 radio and television programs and written over 350 articles for national and international newspapers and magazines.

Ruud S. Jacobs, PhD, is an assistant professor in communication science at the University of Twente, the Netherlands. With a background in media psychology, Dr. Jacobs now investigates persuasive games—digital games that are intended to change players' attitudes. He defended his dissertation "Playing to Win Over: Validating Persuasive Games" at the Erasmus University Rotterdam in 2017. He is also interested in broader mediated forms of persuasion, especially those that are not always recognized as persuasive, such as consumer reviews. Dr. Jacobs lectures in media psychology as well as communication and technology at international bachelor's and master's degree programs at the University of Twente.

Rachel Kowert, PhD, is the Research Director of *Take This,* a nonprofit organization that provides mental health information and resources to gaming communities and the gaming industry. She has been studying games and gamers for more than 10 years, with a specific focus on the social impact of digital game play.

She has published numerous research articles and books on the topic, including *A Parent's Guide to Video Games,* which won an INDIES award in science. For more information on Rachel, and her research, please visit rkowert.com.

Frans Mäyrä, PhD, is a professor of Information Studies and Interactive Media with specialization in digital culture and game studies in Tampere University, Finland. Since 2002, he has been heading the Tampere University Game Research Lab, and he has taught and studied digital culture and games from the early 1990s. He is widely consulted as an expert in socio-cultural issues relating to games, play, and playfulness. His research interests range from game cultures, meaning making through playful interaction, and online social play to borderlines, identity, and transmedial fantasy and science fiction. He is also the director of the Academy of Finland funded Centre of Excellence in Game Culture Studies (2018–2025).

Lis Moberly currently works in the game industry as a writer for Warner Brother's Avalanche in Salt Lake City, Utah. She has worked professionally with streaming platforms for several years and co-created of the first course on video game streaming at the University of Utah with Gabriel Olson in 2019. As a former faculty member of the English and Literature Department at Utah Valley University, Moberly presented and published research on Early Modern philosophy and literature, particularly regarding Giordano Bruno and Margaret Cavendish. She also played a role in the compilation and publication of the Digital Cavendish Project in 2017.

Stephanie Orme, PhD, is an incoming visiting assistant professor of Communication and Media Studies at Emmanuel College in Boston, Massachusetts. She completed her doctorate in Mass Communications at Penn State University, where she specialized in feminist video game studies. Her research examines the global digital gaming industry and gaming culture as they intersect with gender, race, sexuality, class, and disability. She is interested in topics such as "gamer" identity, digital labor, and streaming and esports. She is the current Chair of the Game Studies Division for the National Communication Association, regular speaker at events such as PAXEast and BostonFIG conferences, and an active member of the Boston game development community.

Thorsten Quandt, PhD, is a professor of Online Communication at the University of Münster and a distinguished scientist with extensive experience in digital games research, both nationally and internationally. He is the founding chair of the ECREA section Digital Games Research, and the co-editor of essential books in game studies, like Multiplayer, Multiplayer 2 and The Video Game Debate.

Jessica Stone, PhD, RPT-S, is a licensed psychologist working in a private practice setting in Colorado for more than 25 years. Dr. Stone's interest in therapeutic digital tools, specifically using virtual reality, tablets, and consoles, has culminated in clinical mental health use and research for mental health, medical, and crisis settings. She is the co-creator of the Virtual Sandtray App for iPad (VSA) and the Virtual Sandtray for Virtual Reality (VSA-VR). Dr. Stone has numerous publications to date including *Integrating Technology into Modern Therapies, Game Play, and Digital Play Therapy* and numerous chapters in a variety of books. She has served as the president of the California Association for Play Therapy branch, the Leadership Academy chair, and the Association for Play Therapy Nominations committee and is a member of the AutPlay Advisory Board.

1

REVISITING OLD DEBATES

Rachel Kowert and Thorsten Quandt

Over the last few years, new technologies have been developed and popularized within in the field of game studies. This chapter will provide a (brief) overview of video games, including a summary of the findings and debates of the original *Video Game Debate* volume. This chapter will also reintroduce working definitions of key terms and video games' current position within Western society. In this sense, it will serve both as a connection piece to the previous volume and as a concise overview for readers who are unaware of the discussions covered in the previous book. This chapter will conclude by introducing the debates to be covered within this new volume, including mobile gaming, eSports, gamification, games for change, sex and gender discrimination in games, and games in therapy.

Introduction

Video games are the dominant form of media in the 21st century. Their accessibility and popularity have grown exponentially over the last several decades. Historically, debates about the impact of video games on our physical, mental, and psychological well-being focused on the impact of video game content. Questions around violent video game play, the physical effects of engaging in a predominantly sedentary activity, and video game addiction have typically dominated these discussions. Answering these and other related questions was the focus of the first iteration of *The Video Game Debate* (Kowert & Quandt, 2016). In it, we tackled the most pressing questions regarding video game effects as voiced from scholars, clinicians, policy makers, and parents.

Since the original publication of *The Video Game Debate*, the discourse around video game effects has started to shift away from how the content of games are impacting us and towards how the structure, design, and gaming culture are impacting us. The *Video Game Debate 2* addresses this shift in discourse to address how game design, gaming cultures, novel uses of digital games, and new technologies are impacting our physical, social, and psychological well-being.

However, before we dive in to the new debates within the field, we would like to review the various changes in the field of game studies relating to the debates discussed in the previous volume, including a reintroduction of working definitions of key terms; a discussion about the similarities and differences between video games, online video games, mobile video games, and traditional media; the rise and current state of the video game industry; and video games' current position within Western society. In this sense, it will serve as both a connection piece to the previous volume as well as an overview for those readers who are unfamiliar with the discussion in the previous book. This section will focus on the primary debates tackled in the first volume, including violent video games, video game addiction, and video games and well-being.

Violent Video Games, Aggression, and Violent Crime

Debates about the relationship between violent video games, aggression, and violent crime continue. In February 2020, the American Psychological Association (APA) released a revision to its 2015 resolution on violent crime and video games. In it, they note that violence is a complex social problem that likely stems from many factors. However, just like in the 2015 release, they conclude that there is not enough evidence to conclude whether or not violent video games directly contribute to aggressive and violent outcomes.

Despite the official stance of the APA (2020), delving deeper into the research literature paints a clearer picture. For example, a recently published pre-registered report by Przybylski and Weinstein (2019) concluded that "violent video game engagement, on balance, is not associated with observable variability in adolescents' aggressive behavior" (p. 14). There have also been many studies (not noted by the APA in its resolution) that have found a decrease in violent crime and/or aggression in response to playing violent video games (Ferguson, 2015; Markey, Markey, & French, 2015). Scholars have also noted the importance of context when assessing links between violent video games and aggression and/or violent outcomes. As previously noted by several scholars, when one matches video game conditions more carefully in experimental studies with how they are played in real life, violent video game effects on aggression essential vanish (Ferguson, Miguel, Garza, & Jerabeck, 2011; Przybylski & Weinstein, 2019; Przybylski, Rigby, & Ryan, 2010). Because most video game experiments only have players play for short periods of time, and violent games tend to be more complex than the types of games that are often used as the control condition (such as mobile puzzle games), cutting off play time before the participants have even learned how to play may be creating the post-test increase in aggression (which is actually mislabeled frustration) than the violent content of the game. Knowing this, it is perhaps unsurprising that if players are allowed additional time to learn to play the game, or if researchers provide violent and nonviolent games of equal complexity, the effects disappear (Ferguson et al., 2011; Przybylski & Weinstein, 2019; Przybylski et al., 2010).

Video Game Addiction

In September 2018, the World Health Organization (WHO) announced it would include Gaming Disorder (GD) in the International Classification of Diseases 11th Revision (ICD-11). This decision reinvigorated discussions about the prevalence, etiology, and impact of GD. Today, there remain active debates about how GD should be conceptualized and assessed (Griffiths et al., 2016; Kardefelt-Winther, 2014; Petry et al., 2014). The WHO announcement prompted backlash from the scientific community, which voiced significant concerns about the content of GD as proposed by the ICD-11 due to the low quality research to operationally define and monitor the proposed topic (including a lack of evidence demonstrating the impact of GD on the mental well-being of players), the operational definition of GD relying too heavily upon substance use and gambling disorder criteria, and a lack of consensus on symptomology and assessment of problematic gaming (Aarseth et al., 2017). Mental health professionals have also raised concern that the disordered use of gaming may not be a distinct, unique disorder at all but rather a maladaptive coping strategy for managing other underlying conditions (Boccamazzo, 2019; Kowert, 2019; Schneider, King, & Delfabbro, 2017) Today, there are many critical questions about GD that remained unanswered – specifically, the etiology of GD symptomology and the relationship between GD symptomology and mental health.

However, new developments have indicated that GD may be more of an episodic than chronic condition. Przybylski and Weinstein (2019) found that daily-life, episodic psychological need frustrations (the inability to achieve a sense of autonomy, competence, and control in everyday life) predicted GD symptomology and psychosocial functioning among adolescents. The researchers also found that dysregulated gaming accounted for an insignificant share of variability in psychosocial functioning (measured by a broad assessment of social and emotional functioning) as compared to the role played by basic psychological needs. This suggests that everyday stress and pre-existing psychological challenges significantly fuel behaviors associated with GD symptomology. Although this is the only known study to examine the role of psychological need frustration, the findings are notable as the researchers conclude that knowing the extent to which an adolescent's video-game play has "no practically useful incremental information" (p. 1265).

This research highlights the possibility that disordered use of video games might actually be a management or coping tool for depression and anxiety. These compensation theories (originally developed for research on excessive use of the internet; see Davis, 2001) highlight the motivational role of pre-existing conditions (such as depression and anxiety) in video game involvement (Cole & Griffiths, 2007; Hsu,

Wen, & Wu, 2009; Kowert, 2016). From this perspective, a pre-existing condition within the player, such as depression or anxiety, drives engagement within gaming spaces.

Video Games and Well-Being

There remains a general concern about the impact of video game play on players' well-being, that is, if prolonged video game play undermines physical, social, and mental health (Domahidi, Breuer, Kowert, Festl, & Quandt, 2016; Griffiths et al., 2016; Kardefelt-Winther, 2014; Kaye, Kowert, & Quinn, 2017; Kowert, Vogelgesang, Festl, & Quandt, 2015).

There has been research pinpointing disordered and/or addicted play to increased depression and anxiety (Kim et al., 2016; Scharkow, Festl, & Quandt, 2014) as well as to other poorer mental health outcomes such as lower self-esteem (Stetina, Kothgassner, Lehenbauer, & Kryspin-Exner, 2011) and life satisfaction (Festl, Scharkow, & Quandt, 2012). In 2016, Kim and colleagues found individuals who were classified into a risk group for Internet Gaming Disorder (they met five or more of the nine criteria as outlined by the DSM) scored higher on measures of depression, anxiety, phobic anxiety, interpersonal sensitivity, and hostility, among others.

However, more recently the role of social identity and community has been taken into consideration as a potential "buffer" for these negative outcomes. Kaye and colleagues 2017 found that being a member of the gaming community (as indicated by identifying as adopting the "gamer" social identity) was positively related to self-esteem and social competence. This highlights how identifying with the gaming community can bolster players' sense of well-being, indicating the social value afforded through online forms of digital gaming.

Moving Forward

The impetus to publish *The Video Game Debate 2* was to not only discuss some of the topics that did not receive attention in the first volume (such as gamification and games for change) but also to address the new debates that have arisen within the field of game studies: virtual and augmented reality, the popularization of e-sports, and lootboxes, to name a few.

The remainder of this volume will tackle these new active debates within the field of game studies across eight chapters. This will begin with two chapters related to developments in game design: gamification, loot boxes, and games for change. Each of these chapters will discuss how game design can impact player thoughts and behaviors. This will be followed by three chapters focusing on gamer cultures: discrimination in games, *Twitch* and participatory cultures, and the growth of e-sports. Although some of these facets of gamer culture are not necessarily new, each of these topics has grown to become established fields of study in their own right. As toxic gamer cultures continue unabated, participatory cultures grow in popularity, and e-sports become a multimillion dollar industry, studying their impact is more important than ever. The volume concludes with three chapters discussing novel uses of digital games and new technologies. Because games and learning is a growing area of interest within the field of education, mental health professionals have now started incorporating digital games into therapeutic practice. The use of games in therapeutic settings will be explored, including how the structure of games themselves may be particularly efficacious for certain kinds of psychological intervention. This will be followed by a discussion of virtual and augmented reality, again in the context of therapeutic intervention. Whilst discussions of virtual reality often focus on aspects of playful immersion, there have been many breakthroughs in the use of this technology for educational and therapeutic practice. The volume will conclude with an overview on mobile gaming. From modest beginnings to the saturated market we see today, mobile gaming is arguably the biggest subset of video games currently on the market today. This chapter explores the growth of mobile gaming as well as its potential impact on players and player behavior.

As games continue to shift and evolve, so will our understanding of their uses and effects. This volume will collate what we know about games, gaming, and their effects to provide a greater understanding of how digital games impact our everyday lives today.

References

Aarseth, E., Bean, A. M., Boonen, H., Carras, M. C., Coulson, M., Das, D., … van Rooij, A. (2017). Scholars' open debate paper on the World Health Organization ICD-11 Gaming Disorder proposal. *Journal of Behavioral Addictions*, 6(3), 267–270.

American Psychological Association. (2020). APA Resolution on Violent Video Games. Retrieved from https://www.apa.org/about/policy/resolution-violent-video-games.pdf

Boccamazzo, R. (2019). Gaming Disorder Is a Thing. Now What? Retrieved May 5, 2020, from https://www.takethis.org/2019/05/gaming-disorder-is-a-thing-now-what/.

Cole, H., & Griffiths, M. D. (2007). Social interactions in massively multiplayer online role-playing games. *Cyberpsychology and Behavior*, 10(4), 575–583. Retrieved from https://doi.org/10.1089/cpb.2007.9988.

Davis, R. A. (2001). A cognitive behavioral model of pathologial internet use. *Computers in Human Behavior*, 17(2), 187–195.

Domahidi, E., Breuer, J., Kowert, R., Festl, R., & Quandt, T. (2016). A longitudinal analysis of gaming- and non-gaming-related friendships and social support among social online game players. *Media Psychology*, 21(2), 288–307.

Ferguson, C. J. (2015). Do angry birds make for angry children? A meta-analysis of video game influences on children's and adolescents' aggression, mental health, prosocial behavior, and academic performance. *Perspectives on Psychological Science*, 10(5), 646–666.

Ferguson, C. J., San Miguel, C., Garza, A., & Jerabeck, J. (2011). A longitudinal test of video game violence influences on dating and aggression: A 3-year longitudinal study of adolescents. *Journal of Psychiatric Research*, 46(2), 1–6. Retrieved from https://doi.org/doi:10.1016/j.jpsychires.2011.10.014.

Festl, R., Scharkow, M., & Quandt, T. (2012). Problematic computer game use among adolescents, younger and older adults. *Addiction, 108*(3), 592–599. Retrieved from https://doi.org/10.1111/add.12016.

Griffiths, M. D., Van Rooij, A. J., Kardefelt-Winther, D., Starcevic, V., Kiraly, O., Pallesen, S., … Demetrovics, Z. (2016). Working towards an international consensus on criteria for assessing internet gaming disorder: A critical commentary on Petry et al. (2014). *Addiction, 111*(1), 167–175.

Hsu, S., Wen, M., & Wu, M. (2009). Exploring user experiences as predictors of MMORPG addiction. *Computers and Education, 53*(3), 990–999.

Kardefelt-Winther, D. (2014). A conceptual and methodological critique of internet addiction research: Towards a model of compensatory internet use. *Computers in Human Behavior, 31*, 351–354.

Kaye, L. K., Kowert, R., & Quinn, S. (2017). The role of social identity and online social capital on psychosocial outcomes in MMO players. *Computers in Human Behavior, 74*, 215–223.

Kim, N. R., Hwang, S. S. H., Choi, J. S., Kim, D. J., Demetrovics, Z., Király, O., & Choi, S. W. (2016). Characteristics and psychiatric symptoms of internet gaming disorder among adults using self-reported DSM-5 criteria. *Psychiatry Investigation, 13*(1), 58.

Kowert, R. (2016). Social outcomes: Online game play, social currency, and social ability. In R. Kowert & T. Quandt (Eds.), *The video game debate: Unravelling the physical, social, and psychological effects of digital games* (pp. 94–115). New York: Routledge.

Kowert, R. (2019). Internet gaming disorder: Navigating through the moral panic. Retrieved from https://www.rkowert.com/blog/internet-gaming-disorder-navigating-through-the-moral-panic.

Kowert, R., & Quandt, T. (Eds.) (2016). *The video game debate: Unravelling the physical, social, and psychological effects of digital games*. New York: Routledge.

Kowert, R., Vogelgesang, J., Festl, R., & Quandt, T. (2015). Psychosocial causes and consequences of online video game involvement. *Computers in Human Behavior, 45*, 51–58. Retrieved from https://doi.org/10.1016/j.chb.2014.11.074.

Markey, P. M., Markey, C. N., & French, J. E. (2015). Violent video games and real-world violence: Rhetoric versus data. *Psychology of Popular Media Culture, 4*(4), 277.

Petry, N. M., Rehbein, F., Gentile, D. A., Lemmens, J., Rumpf, H. J., Mößle, T., … Fung, D. S. (2014). An international consensus for assessing internet gaming disorder using the new DSM-5 approach. *Addiction, 109*(9), 1399–1406.

Przybylski, A. K., & Weinstein, N. (2019). Violent video game engagement is not associated with adolescents' aggressive behaviour: Evidence from a registered report. *Royal Society Open Science, 6*(2), 171474. Retrieved from https://doi.org/https://doi.org/10.1098/rsos.171474.

Przybylski, A. K., Rigby, C. S., & Ryan, R. M. (2010). A motivational model of video game engagement. *Review of General Psychology, 14*(2), 154–166.

Scharkow, M., Festl, R., & Quandt, T. (2014). Longitudinal patterns of problematic computer game use among adolescents and adults—A 2-year panel study. *Addiction, 109*(11), 1910–1917.

Schneider, L. A., King, D. L., & Delfabbro, P. H. (2017). Maladaptive coping styles in adolescents with internet gaming disorder symptoms. *International Journal of Mental Health and Addiction, 16*(4), 905–916.

Stetina, B. U., Kothgassner, O. D., Lehenbauer, M., & Kryspin-Exner, I. (2011). Beyond the fascination of online-games: Probing addictive behavior and depression in the world of online-gaming. *Computers in Human Behavior, 27*(1), 473–479.

2

A BRIEF OVERVIEW OF LOOT BOXES IN VIDEO GAMING

Mark D. Griffiths

The buying of loot boxes has received a lot of national and international media publicity. Loot box buying takes place within online gaming and has been described as a virtual game of chance. Players use real money to buy keys to open the boxes, from which they receive a chance selection of virtual items. Many researchers have questioned whether loot box buying is a form of gambling. Depending upon the definition of gambling, the buying of some loot boxes (or equivalents) would arguably be classed as a form of gambling. To date, there has been little research examining loot box buying. Based on the few studies carried out to date, the findings are very consistent that there is an association between problem gambling and loot box buying among both adolescents and adults. However, it is not known whether being a problem gambler increases the likelihood of engaging in loot box buying or whether being a loot box buyer increases the likelihood of problem gambling.

Introduction

Over the past few years, the buying of loot boxes has received a lot of national and international media publicity (e.g., Avard, 2017; BBC, 2019a, 2019b; Griffin, 2019; Griffiths, 2018b; Hood, 2017; Lawrence, 2017). In May 2019, the U.S. Republican senator Josh Hawley said that loot boxes exploit children and should be banned when attempting to pass the Protecting Children from Abusive Games Bill. He was quoted as saying, *"When a game is designed for kids, game developers shouldn't be allowed to monetise addiction. And when kids play games designed for adults, they should be walled off from compulsive micro-transactions"* (BBC 2019b).

What Are Loot Boxes?

Loot box buying primarily takes place within online gaming and depends on both the presence of tradable loot boxes and related winnings within games, plus a marketplace (which can be provided in the game or via dedicated trading platforms). Loot box buying been described as a virtual game of chance (Griffiths, 2018a). Players use real money to buy keys to open the boxes where they receive a chance selection of virtual items. Other types of equivalent in-game virtual assets that can be bought include chests, bundles, crates, card packs, and cases. The virtual in-game items that can be "won" can comprise basic customization (i.e., cosmetic) options for a player's online avatar and in-game assets that can help players progress more effectively in the game (e.g., gameplay improvement items such as armor and weapons) (Drummond and Sauer, 2018; Griffiths, 2018a). Loot box buying is a subset of "microtransactions," an umbrella term comprising in-game purchases (McCaffrey, 2019). According to Schwiddessen and Karius (2018):

> [Microtransactions refer] to a business model … where users can purchase virtual goods via micropayments. … Microtransactions (i.e., premium content) may include downloadable content such as story extensions (so called "DLCs"), additional play time, levels, new maps, virtual currency, weapons, armor, characters, or cosmetic items to customize the player's character or items. The player pays…either directly with real world currency or with some form of fantasy virtual currency (e.g., gold). The latter is typically earned during gameplay or can (often alternatively) be purchased with real world money. (p. 18)

King and Delfabbro (2019) raised concerns concerning in-game micro-transactions such as loot box buying, in particular the predatory monetization and the utilization of individual player data by gaming operators. They claimed,

> [Gaming companies] manipulate the nature and presentation of purchasing offers in ways that maximize the likelihood of the player spending money. Some schemes may exploit an information asymmetry (i.e., the game system knows more about the player than the player can know about the game) to adjust the prices of virtual items for players depending on their playing and spending habits in the game. (p. 1967)

Other tactics to incentivize the purchasing of in-game items is the use of "limited time" offers that attempt to put pressure on gamers to buy such items. Furthermore, most (if not all) gamers are unaware or not informed concerning the odds when buying such in-game items. King and Delfabbro claim that such ploys may exploit gamers (particularly younger individuals) to spend more than they can afford to lose.

In relation to loot box buying, all players hope that they can win "rare" items and are often encouraged to spend more money to do so because the chances of winning such items are minimal (King & Delfabbro, 2018). Many popular video games now feature the chance to buy loot boxes (or equivalents), including *Star Wars Battlefront 2, FIFA Ultimate Team, Overwatch, Middle-Earth: Shadow of War,* and *Lawbreakers* (to name just a few). In short, all of these require the paying of real money in exchange for a completely random in-game item. Psychologist Jamie Madigan (cf. Hood, 2017) asserted that:

> Whenever you open [a loot box], you may get something awesome (or you may get trash). This randomness taps into some of the very fundamental ways our brains work when trying to predict whether or not a good thing will happen. We are particularly excited by unexpected pleasures like a patch of wild berries or an epic skin for our character. This is because our brains are trying to pay attention to and trying to figure out such awesome rewards. But unlike in the real world, these rewards can be completely random (or close enough not to matter) and we can't predict randomness. But the reward system in your brain doesn't know that. Buying [loot boxes] puts them into the same category of packs of Pokémon cards or baseball cards. Unlike gambling in a casino, you're going to get something out of that pack. Maybe just not the thing you wanted. (p. 1)

It should also be noted that loot box buying can have different mechanisms and characteristics (Zendle, Cairns, Barnett, & McCall, 2020), which may have different consequences and psychosocial impacts. The differences include (i) paid and unpaid openings (i.e., in some games players have to pay to open loot boxes and in others they are free to open and are "earned" based upon progressing within the game); (ii) opportunities for cashing out (i.e., the winning content of some loot boxes are not linked to a gamer's account and can be sold on third party sites); (iii) paying to win (i.e., buying loot boxes to help in-game progression); (iv) using in-game currency (i.e., buying loot boxes with in-game currency rather than real money); (v) crate and key mechanics (i.e., earning loot boxes as a result of skillful playing); (vi) showing near-misses (i.e., showing the contents of loot boxes that the player did not choose); and (vii) containing exclusive items (i.e., gaining items that cannot be gained in any other part of the game) (Zendle et al., 2020). The presence or absence of some of these features may also help determine whether the buying of loot boxes is a form of gambling (and will be revisited later in this chapter).

Is Loot Box Buying a Form of Gambling?

For more than 25 years, many scholars have observed that there are behavioral and psychological similarities between gambling and video game playing (e.g.,

Fisher, 1994; Griffiths, 1991, 2005; Griffiths, King & Delfabbro, 2014; King, Delfabbro & Griffiths, 2010a, 2010b). One reason for this is that video games share many of the same structural characteristics as recognized forms of gambling, most notably gaming machines. The term "structural characteristics" refers to those elements of an activity that either induce the person to play or are inducements to continue playing (i.e., characteristics that are responsible for reinforcement may satisfy a player's needs and may actually facilitate playing) (Griffiths, 1993). It has also been observed gambling and gaming technologies have begun to converge, with video games featuring gambling-like elements and gambling games featuring video gaming-like elements (Griffiths et al., 2014). King, Delfabbro, Derevensky & Griffiths (2012) noted that simulated gambling activities and gambling themes have a substantial presence in many modern video games. According to King et al. (2012), gambling content in video games may be categorized according to the following three categories:

- *Standard gambling simulation,* a digitally simulated interactive gambling activity that is structurally identical to the standard format of an established gambling activity, such as blackjack or roulette.
- *Non-standard gambling simulation,* an interactive gambling activity that involves the intentional wagering of in-game credits or other items on an uncertain outcome, in an activity that may be partially modeled on a standard gambling activity but which contains distinct player rules or other structural components that differ from established gambling games.
- *Gambling references,* the appearance of non-interactive gambling material or gambling-related paraphernalia/materials within the context of the video game.

In regard to the second of these categories, it could be argued that the buying of loot boxes is a non-standard gambling simulation. In fact, many researchers have questioned whether loot box buying is a form of gambling (e.g., Brooks & Clark, 2019; Griffiths, 2018a; King & Delfabbro, 2019; Li, Mills & Nower, 2019; Zendle & Cairns, 2018). Although there are many definitions in many disciplines defining gambling, there are a number of common elements that occur in the majority of gambling instances that distinguish "true" gambling from mere risk taking. These include the following: (i) the exchange is determined by a future event, which at the time of staking money (or something of financial value), the outcome is unknown; (ii) the result is determined (at least partly or wholly) by chance; (iii) the reallocation of wealth (i.e., the exchange of money [or something of financial value] usually without the introduction of productive work on either side); (iv) losses incurred can be avoided by simply not taking part in the activity in the first place; and (v) winners gain at the sole expense of losers (Griffiths, 1995, 2015). In addition to the five aforementioned defining features of gambling, Drummond and Sauer (2018) note:

A sixth characteristic that is important to consider is whether the winnings can be converted in some way into real-world money – that is, 'cashed out'. The ability to cash out winnings is often considered a criterion for gambling by regulatory bodies. … Although not all games with loot boxes contain this functionality, some games include the ability to cash out via third party websites (that is, not run by a game company), others via the platform on which the game is distributed. (p. 2)

Added to this, it could be argued that the money or prize to be won should be of greater financial value than the money staked in the first place (Griffiths, 2018a). Based on these elements, the buying of some loot boxes (or equivalents) would arguably be classed as a form of gambling. The UK Gambling Commission's most recent position paper on virtual currencies and social casino gambling (Gambling Commission, 2017) noted the following:

One commonly used method for players to acquire in-game items is through the purchase of keys from the games publisher to unlock 'crates', 'cases' or 'bundles' which contain an unknown quantity and value of in-game items as a prize. The payment of a stake (key) for the opportunity to win a prize (in-game items) determined (or presented as determined) at random bears a close resemblance, for instance, to the playing of a gaming machine. Where there are readily accessible opportunities to cash in or exchange those awarded in-game items for money or money's worth those elements of the game are likely to be considered licensable gambling activities. [Section 3.17] … Additional consumer protection in the form of gambling regulation, is required in circumstances where players are being incentivised to participate in gambling style activities through the provision of prizes of money or money's worth. Where prizes are successfully restricted for use solely within the game, such in-game features would not be licensable gambling, notwithstanding the elements of expenditure and chance. [Section 3.18]

Consequently, the UK Gambling Commission does not consider loot box buying as a form of gambling because (it claims) the in-game items have no real-life value outside of the game. However, this is not the case because there are many websites that allow players to trade in-game items and/or virtual currency for real money. The Gambling Commission appears to acknowledge this point and claim that the buying of in-game loot boxes (and their equivalents) are not gambling but, if third party sites become involved (by allowing the buying and selling of in-game items), the activity does become a form of gambling. As Hood (2017) rightly notes, this appears to be a case of the law struggling to keep pace with technology. There are also issues surrounding age limits and whether games that offer the buying of loot boxes (or equivalents) should be restricted to those over the age of 18 years.

TABLE 2.1 Countries that have considered loot boxes in relation to their gambling regulation

Country	Legal view of buying loot boxes
Australia	The Australian Office of eSafety assert that loot boxes may be a gateway to addictive gambling behavior. However, only the state of Victoria has deemed loot box buying to be a form of gambling.
Belgium	Belgian Gaming Commission has ruled that loot boxes are "games of chance" and come under gambling laws.
China	The Chinese government has said that gaming companies must disclose the odds of winning for loot boxes that are paid for.
Denmark	Danish government have said loot boxes may involve gambling.
Finland	Finland's Lotteries Administration is investigating whether to include loot box buying within its gambling regulation.
France	Autorité de Régulation des Jeux en Ligne does not view buying loot boxes as gambling under their current regulation.
Germany	Loot boxes may violate laws regarding harm and advertising to children.
Holland	The Dutch Gaming Authority has ruled that games where individuals can buy loot boxes with the ability to transfer items are illegal under gambling laws.
Japan	The National Consumer Affairs Agency views virtual items gained from loot box buying as "prizes" even if they have no demonstrable real-world monetary value.
New Zealand	The New Zealand Gambling Commissions does not view buying loot boxes as gambling under its current regulation.
South Korea	The South Korean Fair Trade Commission fined gaming companies in 2018 for misleading odds related to loot box buying. It has requested information from video game developers regarding in-game purchases, particularly related to underage users (April 2019).
Sweden	The Swedish government has said loot boxes may involve gambling.
United Kingdom	The UK Gambling Commission does not view buying loot boxes as gambling under its current regulation.
United States of America	The U.S. Federal Trade Commission is planning to hold a public workshop to examine the video game industry's sale of loot boxes. Proposed bills were in California (failed), Hawaii (failed), Washington (failed), and Minnesota (referred).

Source: Adams (2018); Chalk (2019); Chansky and Okerberg (2019); Kelly (2019); and McCaffrey (2019).

At present, there are a few countries (e.g., Belgium, Holland, and Japan) who do view the buying of loot boxes as a form of gambling (see Table 2.1) and have incorporated such activities into their gambling regulations (Chansky & Okerberg, 2019). To date, only a few jurisdictions have examined whether loot box buying is a form of gambling (see Table 2.1). However, it was reported that gambling regulators from 16 countries were teaming up to examine loot box buying and how to regulate the buying of them (Austria, Czech Republic, France, Gibraltar, Ireland, Isle of Man, Jersey, Latvia, Malta, The Netherlands, Norway, Poland, Portugal, Spain, the United Kingdom, and the United States' Washington State Gambling Commission) (Lanier, 2018). In the main, most countries have either not considered regulating the buying of loot boxes at all or (like the UK and New Zealand) have ruled that buying loot boxes does not currently meet their regulatory definition of gambling (Adams, 2018; Chalk, 2019; Chansky & Okerberg, 2019; Kelly, 2019; McCaffrey, 2019).

Predictably, the gaming industry does not view loot box buying as gambling. For instance, Dirk Bosmans from the European video game rating organization Pan European Game Information (PEGI) stated the following in an interview (cf. Hood, 2017):

> Loot crates are currently not considered gambling: you always get something when you purchase them, even if it's not what you hoped for. For that reason, a loot crate system does not trigger the gambling content descriptor. If something is considered gambling, it needs to follow a very specific set of legislation, which has all kinds of practical consequences for the company that runs it. Therefore, the games that get a PEGI gambling content descriptor either contain content that simulates what is considered gambling or they contain actual gambling with cash payouts. If PEGI would label something as gambling while it is not considered as such from a legal point of view, it would mostly create confusion. We are always monitoring such developments and mapping consumer complaints. We see a growing need for information about specific features in games and apps (social interaction, data sharing, digital purchases), but the challenge is that such features are rapidly becoming ubiquitous in the market, yet they still come in very different shapes and sizes. (p. 1)

Griffiths (2018b) argued that this was somewhat hardline given that PEGI's own descriptor of gambling content is used whenever any video game "teaches or encourages" gambling. Griffiths claimed that such a descriptor arguably covers gambling-like games or activities and that loot box buying is (at the very least) gambling-like. A spokesman for the North American Entertainment Software Rating Board (ESRB) (cf. Hood, 2017) asserted the following:

ESRB does not consider [the buying of loot boxes] to be gambling because the player uses real money to pay for and obtain in-game content. The player is always guaranteed to receive something – even if the player doesn't want what is received. Think of it like opening a pack of collectible cards: sometimes you'll get a brand new, rare card, but other times you'll get a pack full of cards you already have. That said, ESRB does disclose gambling content should it be present in a game via one of two content descriptors: Simulated Gambling (player can gamble without betting or wagering real cash or currency) and Real Gambling (player can gamble, including betting or wagering real cash or currency). Neither of these apply to loot boxes and similar mechanics. (p. 1)

Empirical Studies on Loot Box Buying

To date, there has been little research examining loot box buying. Drummond and Sauer (2018) examined 22 games containing loot boxes from the *Giant Bomb* game review site in 2016 and 2017. Using Griffiths' (1995) five aforementioned criteria for gambling, 10 of the 22 games met all five criteria. Of these ten games, four also gave players the opportunity to cash out winnings (via third party websites that were not affiliated to the gaming company that developed the video game but allowed gamers to trade, buy, and/or sell in-game rewards for real money). Drummond and Saur also noted that the terms of use for playing these four games explicitly stated that reselling or trading virtual currencies was prohibited, but that does not mean that players are unable to do so.

Drummond and Sauer concluded that loot box buying shared both structural and psychological similarities with gambling and that loot box buying sustained player engagement in the game. They also asserted that "of those games containing loot boxes, 100% allow for (if not actively encourage) underage players to engage with these systems" (2018, p. 532). They also noted that although game developers do not appear to be legally responsible for third party websites that allow the trading or reselling of virtual items, such websites facilitate the conversion of in-game items into real currency. Like Griffiths (2018b), they, therefore, argued that loot box buying appears to meet both the legal and psychological definitions of gambling.

A large-scale survey of 7,422 adult gamers by Zendle and Cairns (2018) was the first to examine the relationship between loot box buying and problem gambling (assessed using the Problem Gambling Severity Index [PGSI]). They reported a significant association between problem gambling and the amount of money that gamers spent on buying loot boxes. Based on their findings, the authors went as far as saying that "the gambling-like features of loot boxes are specifically responsible for the observed relationship between problem gambling and spending on loot boxes" (p. 1). However, given the cross-sectional nature of the study, they could not determine whether loot box buying appeals more to problem gamblers than non-problem gamblers or whether loot box buying acts as a "gateway" to problem gambling.

Brooks and Clark (2019) examined the relationships between gaming involvement, loot box buying, and gambling disorder in two small survey studies published in the same paper (144 adults in the first study and 113 university students in the second). Participants completed the Internet Gaming Disorder Scale and the PGSI, as well as answering questions relating to time spent gaming, monthly expenditure, and perceptions concerning the buying of loot boxes. In both studies, the majority of the samples viewed loot box buying as a form of gambling (68.1% in the first study and 86.2% in the second). More than a half had bought loot boxes and approximately one-third had sold a loot box item. Brooks and Clark also created a new measure (the "Risky Loot-box Index" [RLI]) and found that scores on the RLI were significantly associated with problem gambling in both studies.

In an online survey, Li, Mills, and Nower (2019) examined the relationships between problematic gaming (using the American Psychiatric Association's criteria for internet gaming disorder from the *Diagnostic and Statistical Manual for Mental Disorders*), problem gambling (using the PGSI), and loot box buying among a sample of 618 adult video game players. Just under half of the gamers had bought loot boxes (44.2%), and the researchers found that compared to those who had never bought loot boxes, loot box buyers engaged in more online gaming and online gambling more frequently and had higher levels of problem gambling and gaming (as well greater levels of mental distress). Using path analyses, they also demonstrated that loot box buying was directly related to the severity of both problem gambling and problem gaming.

Zendle, Meyer, and Over (2019) examined the relationship between loot box buying and problem gambling (using the Canadian Adolescent Gambling Inventory) in a survey of 1,115 adolescents aged 16–18 years. They reported that the association between loot box buying and problem gambling was stronger than that found among previous studies examining adults. They also reported some qualitative data showing that the reasons for loot box buying were similar to reasons for gambling (e.g., fun and excitement). They concluded by claiming that their "results suggest that loot boxes either cause problem gambling among older adolescents, allow game companies to profit from adolescents with gambling problems for massive monetary rewards, or both" (p. 1).

Zendle et al. (2020) carried out a study on 1,200 participants (61% male, aged 18–40+ years) to determine whether the seven different characteristics and mechanisms of loot box buying (outlined earlier in the chapter) had any associations with problem gambling (again assessed using the PGSI). The results showed a significant positive correlation between (i) loot box spending and problem gambling, (ii) paying for loot boxes and problem gambling, and (iii) loot box spending and problem gambling. The study also found that two loot box characteristics significantly strengthened the relationship between loot box spending and problem gambling (i.e., near-misses and being able to use in-game currency). The study also found that the more money players made from loot boxes, the more severe their gambling problems were.

In November 2018, the UK Gambling Commission published its annual statistics showing that based on a self-report survey of 2,865 children and adolescents aged 11–16 years old, the prevalence of problem gambling had risen to 1.7% (2% for boys and 1.3% for girls) compared to 0.4% in 2016 and 0.9% in 2017 (Gambling Commission, 2018). It was speculated that one of the factors behind the increase may have been the playing of simulated gambling games (or gambling-like activities such as the buying of loot boxes) in video games. The Gambling Commission's (2018) report noted that 13% had played gambling-style games online and that 31% had accessed loot boxes in a video game or app, to try to acquire in-game items.

Macey (2019) surveyed the characteristics of 582 esports spectators who gambled via an international online survey (with 27% of the sample being under the age of 18 years). Participation in gambling and gambling-like activities was found to be 67%, with 4.5% being classed as problem gamblers in the sample using the PGSI. Approximately two-fifths of those who participated in gambling or gambling-like experiences reported that they had bought loot boxes. The study also reported that loot box buying was significantly associated with problem gambling.

Conclusion

Based on the few studies carried out to date, the findings are very consistent that there is an association between problem gambling and loot box buying among both adolescents and adults (and that the association may be even stronger among adolescents). However, it is not known whether being a problem gambler increases the likelihood of engaging in loot box buying or whether being a loot box buyer increases the likelihood of problem gambling because none of the research carried out to date has been longitudinal in nature. Furthermore, all of the empirical research to date has collected self-report data, which are subject to well-known methodological biases (e.g., social desirability, memory recall). Theoretical and conceptual analyses suggest that loot box buying is a form of gambling (or at the very least gambling-like) and that gambling regulators should at least consider whether loot box buying should be examined within a regulatory gambling framework. Governments and regulatory bodies should also consider whether individuals aged under the age of 18 years should be legally allowed to buy loot boxes given the large similarities with more traditional forms of gambling.

References

Adams, R. N. (2018). Finland begins investigating loot box practices. Retrieved August 15, 2019, from https://techraptor.net/content/finland-investigating-loot-box.

Avard, A. (2017). Video games have a loot box fetish, and it's starting to harm the way we play. Games Radar, October 10. Retrieved August 15, 2019, from http://www.gamesradar.com/loot-boxes-shadow-of-war/.

Brooks, G. A., & Clark, L. (2019). Associations between loot box use, problematic gaming and gambling, and gambling-related cognitions. *Addictive Behaviors, 96*, 26–34.

Batchelor, J. (2018). Loot boxes expected to drive games market to $160 billion by 2020. Games Industry, May 1. Retrieved from https://www.gamesindustry.biz/articles/2018-05-01-loot-boxes-expected-to-drive-games-market-to-usd160-billion-by-2022.

BBC. (2019a). EA Games: Loot boxes aren't gambling, they're just like kinder egg. June 20. Retrieved from https://www.bbc.co.uk/news/newsbeat-48701962/.

BBC. (2019b). Loot boxes should be banned, says US senator. May 9. Retrieved from https://www.bbc.co.uk/news/technology-48214293.

Chalk, A. (2019). CS:GO players in Belgium and the Netherlands can no longer open loot cases. *PC Gamer*, July 12. Retrieved August 15, 2019, from https://www.pcgamer.com/uk/csgo-players-in-belgium-and-the-netherlands-can-no-longer-open-loot-cases/.

Chansky, E., & Okerberg, E. (2019). Loot box or Pandora's box? Regulation of treasure chests in video games. *National Law Review*, July 22. Retrieved from https://www.natlawreview.com/article/loot-box-or-pandora-s-box-regulation-treasure-chests-video-games.

Drummond, A., & Sauer, J. D. (2018). Video game loot boxes are psychologically akin to gambling. *Nature Human Behaviour, 2*, 530–532.

Fisher, S. E. (1994). Identifying video game addiction in children and adolescents. *Addictive Behaviors, 19*, 545–553.

Gambling Commission. (2017). *Virtual currencies, esports and social casino gaming – Position paper*. Birmingham, UK: Gambling Commission.

Gambling Commission. (2018). *Young people and gambling*. Birmingham, UK: Gambling Commission.

Griffin, A. (2019). Loot boxes found in Fortnite, Fifa and other games to undergo overhaul. *The Independent*, August 10. Retrieved August 15, 2019, from https://www.independent.co.uk/life-style/gadgets-and-tech/gaming/loot-boxes-fortnite-fifa-odds-chances-rules-uk-a9050176.html.

Griffiths, M. D. (1991). Amusement machine playing in childhood and adolescence: A comparative analysis of video games and fruit machines. *Journal of Adolescence, 14*, 53–73.

Griffiths, M. D. (1993). Fruit machine gambling: The importance of structural characteristics. *Journal of Gambling Studies, 9*, 101–120.

Griffiths, M. D. (1995). *Adolescent gambling*. London, UK: Routledge.

Griffiths, M. D. (2018a). Gambling loot boxes in video games could be conditioning children. *Metro*, December 6. Retrieved August 15, 2019, from https://www.metro.news/gambling-loot-boxes-in-video-games-could-be-conditioning-children/1337389/.

Griffiths, M. D. (2018b). Is the buying of loot boxes in video games a form of gambling or gaming? *Gaming Law Review, 22*(1), 52–54.

Griffiths, M. D., & King, R. (2015). Are mini-games within *RuneScape* gambling or gaming? *Gaming Law Review and Economics, 19*, 64–643.

Griffiths, M. D., King, D. L., & Delfabbro, P. H. (2014). The technological convergence of gambling and gaming practices. In D. C. S. Richard, A. Blaszczynski, & L. Nower

(Eds.), *The Wiley-Blackwell handbook of disordered gambling* (pp. 327–346). Chichester, UK: Wiley.

Hood, V. (2017). Are loot boxes gambling? *Eurogamer*, November 3. Retrieved August 15, 2019, from http://www.eurogamer.net/articles/2017-10-11-are-loot-boxes-gambling.

Kelly, M. (2019). FTC to hold a public workshop on loot box concerns this year. *The Verge*, February 22. Retrieved August 15, 2019, from https://www.theverge.com/2019/2/22/18236352/loot-box-video-game-ftc-workshop-hassan-congress.

King, D. L., & Delfabbro, P. H. (2018). Predatory monetization schemes in video games (eg 'loot boxes') and internet gaming disorder. *Addiction, 113*(11), 1967–1969.

King, D. L., & Delfabbro, P. H. (2019). Video game monetization (eg,'loot boxes'): A blueprint for practical social responsibility measures. *International Journal of Mental Health and Addiction, 17*, 166–179.

King, D. L., Delfabbro, P. H., & Griffiths, M. D. (2010a). Video game structural characteristics: A new psychological taxonomy. *International Journal of Mental Health and Addiction, 8*, 90–106.

King, D. L., Delfabbro, P. H., & Griffiths, M. D. (2010b). The convergence of gambling and digital media: Implications for gambling in young people. *Journal of Gambling Studies, 26*, 175–187.

King, D. L., Delfabbro, P. H., Derevensky, J., & Griffiths, M. D. (2012). A review of Australian classification practices for commercial video games featuring simulated gambling. *International Gambling Studies, 12*, 231–242.

Lanier, L. (2018). Sixteen European, US gambling regulators teaming up to tackle loot boxes, skin gambling. *Variety*, September 17. Retrieved August 15, 2019, from https://variety.com/2018/gaming/news/european-us-gambling-regulators-against-loot-boxes-1202943991/.

Lawrence, N. (2017). The troubling psychology of pay-to-loot systems. IGN, April 23. Retrieved August 15, 2019, from http://uk.ign.com/articles/2017/04/24/the-troubling-psychology-of-pay-to-loot-systems.

Li, W., Mills, D., & Nower, L. (2019). The relationship of loot box purchases to problem video gaming and problem gambling. *Addictive Behaviors, 97*, 27–34.

Macey, J., & Hamari, J. (2019). eSports, skins and loot boxes: Participants, practices and problematic behaviour associated with emergent forms on gambling. *New Media & Society, 21*(1), 20–41. Retrieved from https://doi.org/10.1177/1461444818786216.

McCaffrey, M. (2019). The macro problem of microtransactions: The self-regulatory challenges of video game loot boxes. *Business Horizons, 62*, 483–495.

Schwiddessen, S., & Karius, P. (2018). Watch your loot boxes! – Recent developments and legal assessment in selected key jurisdictions from a gambling law perspective. *Interactive Entertainment Law Review, 1*(1), 17–43.

Zendle, D., & Cairns, P. (2018). Video game loot boxes are linked to problem gambling: Results of a large-scale survey. *PLoS One, 13*(11). e6655.

Zendle, D., Cairns, P., Barnett, H., & McCall, C. (2020). Paying for loot boxes is linked to problem gambling, regardless of specific features like cash-out and pay-to-win. *Computers in Human Behavior, 102*, 181–191.

Zendle, D., Meyer, R., & Over, H. (2019) Adolescents and loot boxes: Links with problem gambling and motivations for purchase. *Royal Society Open Science, 6*(6), 1–18.

3

SERIOUS GAMES: PLAY FOR CHANGE

Ruud S. Jacobs

This chapter describes the state of research into games that have been designed to affect their players beyond offering entertainment experiences. This will include a discussion of the terminology, mechanisms, and effects of serious games. The interdisciplinary nature of the field means that mechanisms are drawn from (media) psychology, computer-human interaction, and educational and communication science while also being rooted in game design principles. The field has not yet yielded validated design principles based on these studies. Apart from the call for standardization and methodological rigor in serious game effect studies, the current chapter offers multiple open questions the field is struggling with. Among others, we need to learn more about the importance of enjoyment and other emotional gratifications, the unique affordances that set games apart from other media, and the generalizability of mechanisms across diverse themes like health, politics, and advertising. These questions need to be addressed before we can say that serious games – as a medium – are equal to or more effective than other (mediated) forms of instruction and persuasion.

In 2019, a charity organization called Jennifer Ann's Group launched *Rispek Danis*, a game aimed at young people in a small island nation in the South Pacific Ocean called Vanuatu. The game takes players through a short story where they learn to perform a dance routine. The three separate moves that make up the rispek danis (in English: respect dance) are less important than the way the dance starts and evolves. Players are told that the rispek danis is not a dance everyone wants to perform all the time; they need to ask for any would-be dance partner's consent before hitting the dance floor. If a dance partner says no, players move on. Though they might try to ask again later, the game notes that consent is not a given. Rather, it is a necessary but not sufficient condition for people to have fun together that no individual dance partner has a right to. It should be obvious that *Rispek Danis* is not a dancing game but a game about teaching the importance of consent to a young audience.

As a stand-alone game that has been developed with the goal to teach players and change their behavior, *Rispek Danis* (Jennifer Ann's Group, 2019) is a serious game. It was a finalist in the 2019 Games for Change (gamesforchange.org) award for games with the "most significant impact," which in this case means its cultural focus on a specific group and its pro-social message were appreciated and considered valid. The label "serious game" is applicable to a growing number of experiences that focus on training, teaching, or persuading their players on virtually any real-world topic (Blumberg, Almonte, Anthony, & Hashimoto, 2013). Although players' enjoyment might be foregrounded by some designers (Bellotti, Kapralos, Lee, Moreno-Ger, & Berta, 2013), it is easy to argue the goal of all serious games is to influence what players know or feel about real-world issues, or even how they behave (Michael & Chen, 2005). Since the medium allows for untold freedom in what kind of game experiences it can offer, the ways serious games are intended to reach this goal are incredibly varied.

Another example of a very popular serious game is *Dumb Ways to Die* (Metro Trains Melbourne, 2013). Developed by the Melbourne metro transit authority as part of a wider campaign to promote safety near railroad tracks and on platforms, *Dumb Ways to Die* shares its primary gameplay conceit with the distinctly non-serious *WarioWare* series (Nintendo, 2003), developed by Nintendo. In both titles, players are subjected to a series of short vignettes where they have to make split-second decisions to earn points. The challenge ramps up quickly as the game speed increases. While the *WarioWare* games are usually about innocuous events like picking one's nose where failure only incurs a loss of points, *Dumb Ways to Die* has much higher stakes. Players who, for example, fail to duck while standing next to a bear will see their character decapitated. Still, apart from cartoonishly gruesome fail states, a train-based main menu, and the odd train-related challenge such as stepping back from a yellow line on a platform, players are not likely to encounter any overt messaging relating to train safety in *Dumb Ways to Die*. The developers have instead split their message across different elements of a multimedia campaign that also includes a viral music video public service announcement. Although there does not seem to be any published work on the effects of *Dumb Ways to Die*, the tongue-in-cheek, irreverent tone of the game itself is arguably more effective at sparking widespread, repeated engagement to keep the campaign fresh in players' minds, rather than changing players' knowledge or behaviors directly (Devlin et al., 2014; Mulcahy, Russell-Bennett, Zainuddin, & Kuhn, 2018). Instead of arguing that *Dumb Ways to Die* is not a serious game because of its reliance on other media for its messaging, the definition of serious games accounts for all possible game experiences that have goals beyond gratifying players on an entertainment or artistic level (Michael & Chen, 2005).

This chapter tries to provide answers for three different questions: What are serious games? How do serious games work? What do we still need to learn about serious games? This chapter will dispel many misconceptions about this particular genre of game to highlight the games' uses and effects as well as discuss the many unanswered questions still held by scholars, scientists, and other researchers.

What's in a Name: Defining Serious Play

Any historical account of gaming includes frequent references to games being created to stave off a loss of morale during periods of famine (McGonigal, 2011) or to communicate worldviews on commerce and war to children and adults alike (Flanagan & Nissenbaum, 2014). At the same time, a number of contemporary commercial digital games such as *Spec Ops: The Line* (Yager Development, 2012) are more famous for what they say about the real world than their entertainment value. If many or even all games can be argued to fit the label of "serious" on some level, then what is the usefulness of this term? The developer's response would be to say that only serious games advertise their primary purpose as exerting influences on players (Ratan & Ritterfeld, 2009). Aside from some fuzzy boundary conditions where intent cannot be established, this differentiates serious games from most commercial-off-the-shelf games. It makes Elizabeth Magie's *The Landlord's Game* (1904), an early precursor to *Monopoly* (Darrow, 1935) that intended to show the evils of real estate capitalism, stand out from the throngs of follow-up versions developed for the mass market by Parker Brothers and Hasbro. While Magie clearly intended for her game to change players' attitudes, it is unlikely Hasbro would argue the same for *Monopoly* – of which the most recent "*Cheater's Edition*" versions seem to celebrate aggressive, dishonest business practices and all-around greed. Although there is some debate on this (Ritterfeld, 2009), it is undoubtedly more practical to distinguish serious games on their intended effects rather than any possible effects they might have on their players after they are tested (Heeter, 2009).

Even when considering intent, many scholars and developers strongly dislike the term "serious game" because of its colloquial use for experiences that are often anything but serious to the player. In their discussion of the term's history, Djaouti and colleagues (2011) consider it an oxymoron that was originally meant to show how the normally inconsequential nature of play can sometimes affect players' lives in ways that are anything but trivial. It was a way to normalize the idea of a game intended for impact on a society that still too often sees the medium as frivolous. This caused some to decry the term as implying that serious games are not enjoyable and call for alternatives (Games4Change Europe, 2011). Although the meaning of the term serious game has in the last two decades all but crystallized into how it is used in this chapter, some competition has indeed emerged; many developers, stakeholders, and researchers prefer the terms games for change, games for impact (or impact games), and applied games. For proponents of these terms, the names denote subtly different points of view: games for change and games for impact are mostly related to pro-social topics (Steinemann et al., 2017), even though the history of serious games means the term also includes titles like *America's Army* (United States Army, 2002) – seen by many as a military recruitment tool (Malliet, Thysen, & Poels, 2011) – as well as games that advertise products and brands. At this stage it is difficult to disentangle which terms were proposed to signal a play experience distinct from serious games and which only served to whitewash the practice of developing games specifically for their effects on players.

More complicated still, many choose to refer to subcategories of serious games over the original term. Among others, these subcategories include educational games (De Grove, van Looy, Neys, & Jansz, 2012), games for learning (Sherry, 2015), game-based learning (All, Núñez Castellar, & Van Looy, 2015), persuasive games (Bogost, 2008), advergames (Cauberghe & De Pelsmacker, 2010), games for health (Kato, 2012), newsgames (Treanor & Mateas, 2009), political games (Neys & Jansz, 2010), and even notgames (Magnuson, 2011). The dizzying array of terms might seem helpful for identifying specific experiences, but they are mostly related to the theme or topic a game focuses on. The underlying mechanisms and broad intended effects (e.g., knowledge or skills gains, attitude or behavior change) are very often shared across themes (Jacobs, Jansz, & de la Hera Conde-Pumpido, 2017; Ratan & Ritterfeld, 2009). A newsgame about slavery practices in cotton picking could use persuasive mechanisms that are identical to those in a game about depression in all but the specific attitudes they were designed to change. Again, the usefulness of the overarching term lies in how it goes beyond topical boundaries to help determine what these experiences have in common and allowing designers to use insights on one theme to improve games on another.

Although the above deliberations are useful for creators and propagators of serious games as discretely designed packages, the picture changes considerably when one takes the educators' and players' perspective. For them, the question whether an individual game is serious or not is moot; as all games could theoretically have positive and negative effects on players, the critical element is how they are used. The process of using a game to teach, train, or persuade oneself or others is referred to as serious gaming (Haring, Chakinska, & Ritterfeld, 2011; Jenkins et al., 2009). Broadly speaking, serious gaming evangelists are divided in two camps. The first sees the primary purpose of serious gaming as motivating players to engage with learning content. They play a game in a didactically encouraging, enthusiastic environment, and to get the most out of their experience, they need to learn relevant information – if not to proceed, then at least to understand what is happening in-game. This optimistic stance requires players to have a need to learn and a willingness to absorb complex information that is not necessarily pertinent to their current task – a willingness not everyone shares (Cacioppo & Petty, 1982).

Another way of looking at serious gaming takes the motivating aspect of games as just one of three possible "serious" use cases of games. De la Hera Conde-Pumpido (2017) called this aspect endocentric persuasion, for its tendency to pull players further and deeper into a game experience. While this use case does not require the specially designed serious games discussed earlier, endocentric persuasion can only ever draw players toward whatever is in the game or play experience. In this sense, playing *Pokémon Go* (Niantic, 2016) can, along with many other titles, be considered serious gaming in how players are motivated to go outside and interact with others as part of its gameplay. The benefits for players of games that are endocentrically persuasive are inherent to the experience of the game. The second use case of serious gaming involves the use of games that are purpose-built to train, teach, or persuade – the last of which is referred to as exocentric persuasion for persuasive games (de la Hera Conde-Pumpido, 2017). These games fit the definition of serious games as discussed in this chapter. For example, the use case of *Rispek Danis* (Jennifer Ann's Group, 2019) depends on its exocentric persuasion, as it needs to change players' attitudes on the importance of consent in the real world through its narrative and gameplay messages.

A third form of serious gaming uses games that are recognized as having some kind of serious influence but that were not necessarily designed as such. If every game can be thought of as having something to say about the real world, game-mediated persuasion (de la Hera Conde-Pumpido, 2017) describes the process by which those messages can be recognized. Especially in educational settings, game-mediated serious play involves selecting a commercial off-the-shelf game and playing it in group-based settings before starting a discussion (Breuer & Bente, 2010). Charsky and Mims (2008) give specific guidelines to educators looking to involve commercial off-the-shelf games in their teaching. They describe the *Civilization* (MicroProse, 1991) and *SimCity* (Maxis, 1989) series as interesting simulations of history and city planning, respectively, while advising educators using these games to challenge players to find this bias and reflect on it. The discussion stage, also referred to as debriefing (Erb, 2015), is useful for any kind of serious gaming but especially helps to contextualize players' experiences with entertainment games by allowing disclaimers for parts of the game that are inaccurate and combining insights from different experiences with the game that individual players might not have picked up on. Game-mediated forms of serious gaming are still relatively rare in formal educational settings, partly because educators do not always see the value of it (Stieler-Hunt & Jones, 2017) but also because of the difficulty in selecting a fitting title. One way to mitigate the dangers of using commercial titles is to modify (or "mod") the game, for example, by tweaking its scenarios or changing certain rules (Soflano, 2011). This is often a time-intensive process and requires varying levels of experience depending on the title and nature of the modification. Of course, the more effort it would cost to mod a game to fit into an existing curriculum, the better off an educator would be with a purpose-built serious game.

Serious games have one more terminological hurdle to clear: anyone unfamiliar with games is very likely to confuse serious games with *gamification*. Although gamification is discussed and critiqued in more detail by Espen Aarseth (this volume), the ways serious games set themselves apart from this process deserves mention here. After all, both tend to involve the use of elements of games to change players' knowledge, attitude, or behavior, and so both could be employed for similar goals. Gamification also relies on the previously discussed endocentric persuasion (de la Hera Conde-Pumpido, 2017) to keep users motivated to complete tasks. But where gamification involves an overlay of game-like elements on real-world tasks and transforming the reward structure or motivation around it, serious games tend to isolate tasks to the game environment, expecting players to transfer any influences out of their experience with the games. Serious games are also more self-directing, especially in education: "serious games are typically designed to fulfill the role of instructor by actually providing instructional content to learners, whereas gamification is designed to augment or support pre-existing instructional content" (Landers, 2014, pp. 764–765). For instance, where a gamified surgical training tool might award students points for completing sections or show their comparative progress on a leaderboard to motivate repeated use, the game *Underground* (Grendel Games, 2015), discussed later in this chapter, replaces the tool altogether and transforms the setting to a sci-fi-themed adventure that nevertheless lets players hone the same skills they need to perform surgical procedures (Goris, Jalink, & ten Cate Hoedemaker, 2014).

Unsurprisingly, the line between gamification and serious games is often blurred. At first glance the running app *Zombies, Run!* (Six to Start, 2012) can be described as gamified because of how it elevates the practice of running using game-like elements: it applies the trope of being chased by a zombie horde to spur users to run, and running certain distances yields resources that can be used in a base-building metagame. Deeper engagement with the app reveals that it does more than just layer reward structures over the act of running. Players are submerged in a serious game world conveyed almost entirely through sound in which their athleticism is both the main input channel as well as the product of playing regularly (Witkowski, 2013).

Ultimately, the discussion of when a game is a serious game is nearly always academic and the medium is doing fine despite its fuzzy boundaries. With its fictionalized war-torn setting and multi-platform commercial distribution, *This War of Mine* (11 bit studios, 2014) falls outside the typical range of serious games (Ratan & Ritterfeld, 2009). Still, there is little doubt over the developer's intent to affect players' perceptions of life during wartime beyond their time with the game (de Smale, Kors, & Sandovar, 2019). Developers can still take pointers from its design (Sterczewski, 2016), and educators could select it for their contemporary history curriculum – albeit with some caveats (Šisler, 2016). The same holds true for Lukas Pope's ludography (dukope.com), which comfortably straddles the lines between serious and commercial, educational and entertaining.

The Sea Has No Claim (Pope, 2014) is a free game that educates players on the difficulty of finding planes that disappear during ocean flights, having been developed shortly after Malaysia Airlines flight 370 mysteriously went down on March 8, 2014. The simulation of border customs in a fictional Eastern Bloc country in *Papers Please* (3909 LLC, 2013) is less overtly educational – and sold on multiple platforms – but its critical perspective on the accountability that individuals within a larger regime have is difficult to ignore (Peña, Hernández Pérez, Khan, & Cano Gómez, 2018). With games like this it is perhaps more useful to derive their "seriousness" from the effects they have on players (Ritterfeld, 2009).

Types of Mechanisms and Effects

Once someone decides to develop a serious game, the array of different effects, mechanisms in games that can achieve these effects, and approaches to development could feel dizzying. Digital games[1] enable a message sender to use all the depth of other audiovisual media, including text, images, sounds, animations, and narratives, which can combine to staggering effect with elements unique to games, such as players' agency and the possibility of generating immediate feedback to player actions. Serious games often use these elements in completely unique combinations, and it is rare to see even games that broach the same topic doing so in similar ways. As the many games developed to combat teen dating violence published by Jennifer Ann's Group (Crecente, 2014) demonstrate, serious games are almost always the product of the personal view of a designer on a topic and what aspect of it to approach from a gameplay perspective (Jacobs, Kneer, & Jansz, 2019). In response, there is a growing number of player-centered theories of how these games work.

The following section will overview a few examples of these theories and effects demonstrated in empirical studies in recent years, following a broad-level distinction between games that teach or educate, games that train or develop skills, and games that persuade or change behaviors. Games will be separated between those that that primarily intend for cognitive effects (i.e., semantic, declarative, and strategic knowledge); games that foster physical and mental abilities (including motor skills and procedural knowledge); and games that aim for an affective impact on beliefs and attitudes (Garris, Ahlers, & Driskell, 2002). This is not to say that any serious game only does one of these things; most serious games have some aspects of all three.

Educating and Teaching

In the predecessor to this volume, John Sherry proposed that there might be "too many visions and not enough action" (Sherry, 2015, p. 129) in the world of evidence-based educational game design. As might be obvious from the many different terms in use for playful educational experiences, the comparatively larger amount of academic attention paid to educational games when compared to persuasive and training games has not necessarily translated into a firm empirical basis to fuel design efforts. The headless enthusiasm is understandable; games have not yet fully shed their image as a medium for children, and educators outside games at least see the motivating potential of games. The fact that selecting or developing the right game is such a challenge only increases interest of external parties looking to harness gaming for good. To be fair, several pockets of researchers have recently started to meaningfully validate their effects using systematic theories of learning (All, Núñez Castellar, & Van Looy, 2016; Bellotti et al., 2013). The work continues apace, but readers should not expect a one-size-fits-all effect mechanism for learning.

One efficacious strategy has been to look at serious games as elaborate forms of instructional design. Games have players dive into an issue in a practical way, assuming a role in a simulated slice of reality to see how it works (Garris et al., 2002). Games naturally adhere to many rules of instructional design. Information can be presented concurrently in audio and visual channels, which maximizes the amount of information that can be processed (Annetta, 2010). Players enact what they are learning immediately. Games tend to encourage exploration and let players make mistakes. Instant feedback is given to ensure players can see whether they understood what they learned. Games also tend to gate progress with puzzles, boss battles, and other gauntlets that inherently test players for their understanding before proceeding. This gives educators the opportunity to seamlessly integrate assessment of students in the game's design (Annetta, 2010; Bellotti et al., 2013).

One concern appears when considering games from an instructional design perspective. Games are frequently (though not always fittingly) associated with the experience of flow, a state of focused activity where challenge and skill are matched, and with frenetic gameplay, both of which could be detrimental to any learning effects (Adams & Clark, 2014). If players are too busy playing the game, their so-called cognitive load is too high to accommodate learning. Theories of cognitive load model our capacity to pay attention to things, elaborate on our thoughts, and store away information in memory. Cognitive load creates a problem especially for game designers operating under the assumption that serious games always need to be "fun" to play. The focus on fun or "entertainment" is seen by many as inherent to digital game-based learning (All et al., 2016; Spagnolli, Chittaro, & Gamberini, 2016). Designers making fun games first place the intended effects second, and possibly include them only after the gameplay types have been determined. This can cause some games to overload players with their gameplay and stop them from absorbing the rest of the game's messaging (DeSmet et al., 2014; Woo, 2014). Of course, this view is obsolete. It is perfectly possible to embed a message in the way a game is played (more on this later), meaning that cognitive load is intrinsically linked to processing this message

(Adams & Clark, 2014). Especially when it comes to sensitive topics, this design approach does require some extra thought to get right, as the recent public outcry around "slave *Tetris*" demonstrated (Mukherjee, 2016). Clearly, not every subject can – or maybe should – be embedded in traditional gameplay mechanics.

If instructional design seems too sterile and digital game-based learning relies too much on combining existing gameplay with learning strategies, there is always the media-driven approach. Taking cues from educational efforts in traditional media, the motivation to learn can also be evoked through identification or engagement with game protagonists. One well-publicized educational game to attempt this is *Poverty Is Not a Game* (*PING*, iMinds, 2010). Using adventure gameplay with minor role-playing elements, players step into the shoes of a newly homeless young adult and make choices on where to go, what jobs to apply for, and even what to eat. Its learning effects were driven at least in part by players' identification with the protagonist. Instead of coolly choosing optimal paths through the game, players saw themselves as like the impoverished main character (De Grove et al., 2012). Perhaps surprisingly, players felt they learned more when they played the game in private settings at home than in a group setting at school (De Grove et al., 2012), though this was partly traced back to differences in technical capabilities of school computers and longer play sessions at home. Clearly, the context in which games are played matter to how they can impact players.

Overall, there is widespread recognition that learning games do indeed have benefits for knowledge acquisition and some forms of behavioral change (Connolly, Boyle, MacArthur, Hainey, & Boyle, 2012). The sub-domain of health-related learning games show these same effects, with similar caution for long-term behavioral change (DeSmet et al., 2014). The call for more rigor in assessing effects by Sherry (2015) is echoed as well, indicating that researchers (approaching the topic from different angles) are not used to applying uniform validation mechanisms (All, Nunez Castellar, & Van Looy, 2014; Kato, 2012; Van Oostendorp, Warmelink, & Jacobs, 2016). True, methodological opportunism abounds, but this is predominantly coming from researchers outside of social sciences. The uptick in more rigorous validation studies is promising, but we are still some way off from validating how individual mechanisms in games improve learning. The broad application areas and seemingly endless bandwidth of games make this even more difficult.

Training and Skill Development

The above considerations apply mostly to declarative knowledge gains. Skill development, on the other hand, is a less conscious process that tends to involve more repetition and requires players to transfer the behaviors they learned into real-world settings. Skill development can be separated into motor skills – the movements themselves – and procedural knowledge of what actions to take. Both of these are hard to verbalize, but the cognitive basis of procedural knowledge makes it easier to express using off-the-shelf technology. Consider *abcdeSIM* (Erasmus University Medical Center & IJsfontein, 2013), a medical training game that simulates the challenges of working in a hospital emergency room (Dankbaar et al., 2016a). Rather than practicing surgical or other physical skills themselves, *abcdeSIM* centers on rapid decision-making. Players can call on various indicators of their patients' states to diagnose and treat them. Their actions (or inaction) are reflected in state changes that are modeled based on medical data. It should not come as a surprise, then, that this game was also based on instructional design principles (Faber, Dankbaar, & van Merrienboer, 2018). The intent to increase confidence in real-life emergency situations by forcing students to repeat and streamline in-game decision-making behaviors under time pressure is what sets this type of experience apart from other learning games (Dankbaar et al., 2016b). Seen in this way, both *Rispek Danis* (Jennifer Ann's Group, 2019) and *Dumb Ways to Die* (Metro Trains Melbourne, 2013) are essentially skill training games: they repeatedly force players through simple choices (i.e., requesting consent for intimate contact and shielding oneself from harm) so that these choices become rote in interactions outside the games. The mechanism for rote repetition games' effects is akin to that of fire drills – a realization that makes the existence of fire drill games (Rüppel & Schatz, 2011) rather unsurprising.

While standard serious game delivery methods (being desktop and laptop computers and tablets) are potential vectors of procedural learning, their standardized input mechanisms limit the scope of what motor skills they can impart. Beyond general positive effects on cognition and precision motor skills (Granic, Lobel, & Engels, 2013; Wouters, van der Spek, & van Oostendorp, 2009), only a few skills with real-world applications (e.g., typing) can be directly translated from touch screens, game controllers, or a keyboard and mouse. This means that serious games teaching motor skills are often built around their interaction methods. Although they have been around for decades in the form of simulators that teach skills like aircraft control and surgery (Satava, 1993), few would call these devices games. Apart from some efforts to gamify progress or introduce competitive elements, simulators have been rather dry. Quite recently, developers have started incorporating more ludic elements in skill training. One example of this is Grendel Games' *Underground* (2015), a game played on a slightly modified Nintendo Wii-U game console that trains laparoscopic surgical skills. This specific form of surgery is tricky to learn because the small opening the tools pass through on the patient's body invert the surgeon's movements. By integrating Wii remotes (off-the-shelf motion controllers) into simple plastic facsimiles of surgical tools, *Underground*'s creators have created an inexpensive, easily scalable simulation that nevertheless affords adequate precision (Overtoom et al., 2017). Chiefly, however, *Underground* surpasses straightforward simulators by transplanting its setting from medical to science fiction; players control robot arms that manipulate and remove impediments in a dark cavern. Players spent more time performing motions in this fantastical setting (Goris et al., 2014) while the rate of basic skill development was comparable to that of previously validated simulators (IJgosse, van Goor, & Luursema, 2018).

Skill development games are sold less on their ability to attain the precision of simulators or the total experience of real-life practice and more on their ability to motivate players. Since spending time with one of these games ought to be inherently tied to skill improvement, their designs are best geared toward maximizing contact. This is achieved mostly through gamification, adding engaging characters or narratives, or designing interesting themes to liven up otherwise boringly repetitive actions. All these endeavors could end up excluding as many players as are drawn in. Identification with protagonists drives continued play and enjoyment for some players, but those players then react negatively to being given external rewards (Birk, Mandryk, & Atkins, 2016). Acceptance of serious games is also related to what kind of gaming aptitude they require from their players, especially among (older) adults (Vidani, Chittaro, & Carchietti, 2010). Designers should consider their players' age and familiarity with technology at an early stage for this to inform a game's format and broad-strokes visual design.

Not all games where players practice certain motor movements or procedural knowledge are intended to improve those skills. As part of a wider range of games that use physical restrictions to simulate disabilities (Pivik, McComas, Macfarlane, & Laflamme, 2002), playing *Birthday Party* involves a proprietary wheelchair-based control system (Gerling, Mandryk, Birk, Miller, & Orji, 2014). The embodied virtual reality experience *A Breathtaking Journey* (Eindhoven University of Technology, 2015) casts players as a refugee hiding in a truck as they are traveling to Europe – and even forces players to hold their breath to avoid getting caught (Kors, Ferri, van der Spek, Ketel, & Schouten, 2016). The intended outcome of these games is not to improve players' wheelchair prowess or lung capacity but rather to have them behave and think like another person. These games mean to increase empathy, perspective-taking, or simply change attitudes towards the topic under discussion. In other words, these are persuasive games.

Persuasion and Behavior Change

Persuasion is distinct from knowledge and skill development in two ways. First, the intended change is attitudinal, which means persuasive games aim to affect how people feel about a person, issue, or object. Despite frequent allusions to impacting behavior, persuasion does not necessarily involve behavior change and behavior change from serious games necessarily results at least partly from attitude change. Second, although few would fault the idea of cultivating knowledge and skills in players, persuasive effects are not necessarily pro-social. Next to the games promoting empathy and perspective-taking (e.g., Peng, Lee, & Heeter, 2010), a large swath of persuasive games instead advertises brands and products (Waiguny, Nelson, & Marko, 2013), and a few others actively promote hatred

(Daniels & Lalone, 2012). Although I do argue there are some specific differences between advergames and other persuasive games in their principal mechanism for attitude change (Jacobs, 2017, sec. 1.2.2), any study showing the effects of "the good" also could propagate "the bad." The focus here is on the way games can set players to elaborate on a game-based message to come to their own conclusions, rather than looking at more subversive, stealthy processes (e.g., as discussed by Kaufman, Flanagan, & Seidman, 2016).

On a theoretical level, cognitive load is a critical factor for serious games. For persuasive games, cognitive load (i.e., the amount of mental resources that are allocated to performing a task at any given time) is one of a few elements that can determine whether players can and will give their attention to any persuasive messages. Ability to elaborate is impacted along similar lines in persuasive games as knowledge consolidation is in learning games. When cognitive load during play is high, players have more trouble recalling the game's message (Vyvey, Núñez Castellar, & Van Looy, 2018). According to several theories of persuasion (such as the elaboration likelihood model, Petty & Wegener, 1999), players would also need to be motivated to elaborate on a message.

One way in which both motivation and ability can be influenced at the same time is through procedural rhetoric (Bogost, 2008). This concept describes an intertwining of a game's message and the systems and rules that make up its gameplay. Games with procedural rhetoric essentially have players playing the message itself. Consider *My Cotton Picking Life* (Rawlings, 2012), a game that tasks players with picking a vast amount of cotton. The game pushes a bleak audiovisual experience on players, and some text before and after play makes its message explicit with regards to the inhumane conditions under which people in Uzbekistan are being exploited in cotton picking fields (Jacobs et al., 2017). After comparing the game's effects to a YouTube video on the same topic, however, the game's effects on players' attitudes toward the physical labor of picking cotton were more pronounced than those of the video (Jacobs, 2018). The choices to persist or give up are especially poignant because of the game's simple system where each picking action only yields a realistically small amount of cotton. In fact, by testing the original game against versions in which the cotton picking quota are easily achieved, we found that the game's persuasive message relies very strongly on this one aspect of play (Jacobs, 2017, Chapter 7). Despite ostensibly being as deep as any product of a game jam, *My Cotton Picking Life* employed a simple procedural rhetoric on the futility and endlessness of picking cotton that nevertheless was responsible for the bulk of its persuasive effect. One important question is left before procedural rhetoric can be seen as a viable persuasive mechanism: Is elaboration on game-based messages dependent on keeping cognitive load at a manageable level? Put another way, as players are forced to take another's perspective at least for the duration of play (Juul, 2013), does this not mean that any cognitive load is directly invested in elaborating on that perspective?

Procedural rhetoric is just one of multiple persuasive dimensions in games (de la Hera Conde-Pumpido, 2015). We should also take more holistic approaches into account that aim for a certain player experience. Several game researchers consider attitude change a result of affective learning (Wouters et al., 2009), which also entails increased motivation. Ruggiero's (2015) study on *Spent,* a persuasive game about homelessness, shows players' positive attitudes endured longer than those of participants who read a text about the same topic. The game also led to higher scores on an affective learning scale, though it is unclear what this means for the overall player experience (Iacovides & Cox, 2015). It is likely that the motivational impact of affective learning depends on appreciation of a game's narrative and identification with its characters (Steinemann et al., 2017). From this angle, persuasive games are forms of entertainment-education that thrive on a connection with a protagonist who is in the process of changing his or her attitude (Slater, 2002). Players' attitude change would then reflect the new insights gained by the protagonist. We found some evidence for this when studying games about dating violence, in that a game with a stages-of-change narrative (called *Another Chance,* Another Kind, 2015) changed certain attitudes regarding the acceptability of abusive behaviors (Jacobs et al., 2019). Surprisingly, this game seemed to have the same effects on attitudes as a much shorter game that relied more on its gameplay than its narrative.

While it is too soon to say that all persuasive dimensions affect players in equal measure, it does seem like designers are (to some extent) free to choose a mechanism that fits the message. I would even argue that designers should (and do: Jacobs et al., 2017) question their base assumptions about what makes a good game. Serious game design pursues different goals than entertainment game design; the latter imposes unnecessary constraints on game experiences. As an example, consider the unwritten rule that games always need to be winnable. Ruggiero and Becker (2015) show that making a game unbeatable could serve as an accurate reflection of a real-world issue, depending on a game's message. As discussed before, *My Cotton Picking Life* (Rawlings, 2012) was considerably less persuasive when it let players reach short-term goals easily because the message of the game was predicated on the futility and endlessness of forced labor. In the end, the game's message should be prioritized over notions of playability.

In All Seriousness: Unanswered Questions in Serious Games

Serious game developers and researchers are divided on whether the medium has a duty to entertain players or not. As might be clear from the last section, many scholars tend to only consider entertainment value as relevant insofar as it is in service of a game's message or goal (Crutzen, van't Riet, & Short, 2015; Elson, Breuer, Ivory, & Quandt, 2014; Iten & Petko, 2016; Vyvey et al., 2018). However, what is still needed is a more nuanced interpretation of vague terms such as enjoyment, fun, and entertainment. *This War of Mine*'s (11 bit studios,

2014) designers did not feel compelled to make players laugh. Instead, they aimed for emotional realism (de Smale et al., 2019). Games can elicit appreciation through meta-emotions, which have long been considered an important driver for consumption of media in general (Oliver & Bartsch, 2010). After repeated anomalous results with regard to player enjoyment of the games, a multi-dimensional scale for persuasive game experiences has been proposed that includes questions about how players enjoyed learning and growing as a person, among others (Jacobs, 2017, Chapter 8). Early results with this scale are informative, but additional questions remain. Moving forward, it will be important to understand players' levels of enjoyment for serious games across settings; how players include the labeling of these games as intending to train, teach, or persuade in their appreciation; and how appreciation relates to motivation to keep playing, among many others.

The emphasis many researchers place on games being fun stems from the notion that only fun games attract audiences. Pointing to the popularity of *Dumb Ways to Die* (Metro Trains Melbourne, 2013), one could argue that the cheerful outward appearance and darkly comedic gameplay were mostly responsible for its ability to reach its immense audience. In truth, we know very little about the acceptance and diffusion of serious games. Vidani et al. (2010) offers ideas on what could make nurses more accepting of skills training games, saying that training in game form is better suited to broad-strokes introductions to these skills. A research line headed by Jeroen Bourgonjon shows the complexity of this issue by querying students, parents, and teachers separately. Parents are more likely to agree to their children playing serious games if they recognize the learning opportunity and perceive norms around games as positive (Bourgonjon, Valcke, Soetaert, de Wever, & Schellens, 2011). The teachers share these beliefs but also base their stance toward games in their classrooms on their perceived usefulness (Bourgonjon et al., 2013). Finally, students rely on their experiences with games in other settings to predict games' ease of use and usefulness (Bourgonjon, Valcke, Soetaert, & Schellens, 2010). Of course, this research only offers a snapshot of initial acceptance by audiences that were asked or even required to play. How the games are integrated into educational curricula and how important facets such as debriefing are handled are not currently known. We know even less about how people come to the decisions to start, continue, and finish playing serious games in their free time. This is surprising, given the sheer volume of games that are available online in HTML and app form. Before we can determine that serious games are validated as a medium, we need to know how they attract players and which groups are *not* playing serious games. The last question is especially poignant because it can show whether serious games are simply "effective at preaching to the choir of already engaged youth" (Raphael, Bachen, Lynn, Baldwin-Philippi, & McKee, 2010, p. 226) or if they are engaging new audiences. Considering the current state of validation through effect studies, finding determinants of game acceptance and appropriation would yield much more interesting insights about the medium at large – at this stage – than studies on captive study participants.

So far, serious game research has been led by the zeal of designers. Noting that validation is lagging, interdisciplinary researchers have compensated by proposing a large number of theories, models, and mechanisms to explain games' effects – only a few of which were discussed here. Rather than increasing effect studies' rigor, this has partitioned the medium into different themes, technologies, or intended effects. Even though we should be doing more to push the validation of the medium as a whole forward, the different types of effects described above underline that there will not (nor should there) be a unified validation method for all serious games. Instead, we should work toward validating individual mechanisms of effects across themes. After all, a designer working on health games with narratives can use the results of Steinemann et al. (2017) on interactive narratives in much the same way as one developing political games in virtual reality. With the exception of games that intend medical benefits, we should not want to validate each individual game with randomized controlled trials. This is not required of every new television commercial or educational textbook. Serious games need a firm evidence base of additive benefits of game elements and – if designers were not able to take a human-centered design approach – quality assessment and usability testing on par with competing media's focus groups. Developers need to set aside time and effort for the latter, while researchers can work on the former.

We are not at this stage yet, though. Serious games are still side-eyed by many parties as either frivolous or subversive. Fans of commercial games, still defensive as a result of the violence debate (Coulson & Ferguson, 2015), might even deny games affect players at all. To allow games to have positive effects, we acknowledge they also might have some adverse effects. Fortunately, this is based on a false equivalence: violent games are not intended to make their players violent, while serious games are purpose-built to change players. Even the oft-maligned rampage game *Hatred* (Destructive Creations, 2015), which seems to have been intended for shock value and infamy, does not claim to teach or encourage players to copy the game's violence in the real world. There is a long way to go before the term "evidence-based" can be used across all serious games, but their effects are at least implemented intentionally and explicitly based on designers' experience and creativity. Although this distinction is by itself not evidence against negative behavioral effects of commercial games, it is a reasonable explanation for the differences in effects reported between violent entertainment games and most kinds of serious games. A mature medium is considered neither a magic bullet nor trivially inert. As we slowly settle into a nuanced understanding of what play means in the 21st century, we need to consider games as a medium of communication that can be as serious as its creators want it to be.

Note

1 Many forms of serious gaming, in fact, do not make use of digital games at all and instead focus on social, role-based, or board-based forms of play. These types of co-located and pervasive serious games have their own benefits and drawbacks and can in some instances be highly impactful. They are not discussed in this chapter.

References

11 bit studios 2014 11 bit studios. (2014). *This War of Mine*. 11 bit studios.

3909 LLC. (2013). *Papers, Please. 3909 LLC*.

Adams, D. M., & Clark, D. B. (2014). Integrating self-explanation functionality into a complex game environment: Keeping gaming in motion. *Computers and Education, 73*, 149–159. Retrieved from https://doi.org/10.1016/j.compedu.2014.01.002.

All, A., Nunez Castellar, E. P., & Van Looy, J. (2014). Measuring effectiveness in digital game-based learning: A methodological review. *International Journal of Serious Games, 1*(2), 3–20. Retrieved from https://doi.org/10.17083/ijsg.v1i2.18.

All, A., Núñez Castellar, E. P., & Van Looy, J. (2015). Towards a conceptual framework for assessing the effectiveness of digital game-based learning. *Computers & Education, 88*, 29–37. Retrieved from https://doi.org/10.1016/j.compedu.2015.04.012.

All, A., Núñez Castellar, E. P., & Van Looy, J. (2016). Assessing the effectiveness of digital game-based learning: Best practices. *Computers & Education, 92–93*, 90–103. Retrieved from https://doi.org/10.1016/j.compedu.2015.10.007.

Annetta, L. A. (2010). The "I's" have it: A framework for serious educational game design. *Review of General Psychology, 14*(2), 105–112.

Another Kind. (2015). *Another Chance*. Jennifer Ann's Group. Atlanta, GA. Retrieved from https://jagga.me/anotherchance.

Bellotti, F., Kapralos, B., Lee, K., Moreno-Ger, P., & Berta, R. (2013). Assessment in and of serious games: An overview. *Advances in Human-Computer Interaction, 2013*, 1–11. Retrieved from https://doi.org/10.1155/2013/136864.

Birk, M. V., Mandryk, R. L., & Atkins, C. (2016). The motivational push of games: The interplay of intrinsic motivation and external rewards in games for training. In *Proceedings of the 2016 Annual Symposium on Computer-Human Interaction in Play – CHI PLAY '16* (pp. 291–303). New York, New York, USA: ACM Press. Retrieved from https://doi.org/10.1145/2967934.2968091.

Blumberg, F. C., Almonte, D. E., Anthony, J. S., & Hashimoto, N. (2013). Serious games: What are they? What do they do? Why should we play them? *The Oxford Handbook of Media Psychology*, 334–351. Retrieved from https://doi.org/10.1093/oxfordhb/9780195398809.013.0019.

Bogost, I. (2008). *Persuasive Games*. Cambridge, Massachusetts: MIT Press. Retrieved from http://www.gamasutra.com/view/feature/3652/persuasive_games_texture.php?print=1.

Bourgonjon, J., De Grove, F., De Smet, C., Van Looy, J., Soetaert, R., & Valcke, M. (2013). Acceptance of game-based learning by secondary school teachers. *Computers & Education, 67*, 21–35. Retrieved from https://doi.org/10.1016/j.compedu.2013.02.010.

Bourgonjon, J., Valcke, M., Soetaert, R., de Wever, B., & Schellens, T. (2011). Parental acceptance of digital game-based learning. *Computers & Education, 57*(1), 1434–1444. Retrieved from https://doi.org/10.1016/j.compedu.2010.12.012.

Bourgonjon, J., Valcke, M., Soetaert, R., & Schellens, T. (2010). Students' perceptions about the use of video games in the classroom. *Computers & Education, 54*(4), 1145–1156. Retrieved from https://doi.org/10.1016/j.compedu.2009.10.022.

Breuer, J., & Bente, G. (2010). Why so serious? On the relation of serious games and learning. *Journal for Computer Game Culture, 4 (1)*, 7–24. Retrieved from https://hal. archives-ouvertes.fr/hal-00692052.

Cacioppo, J. T., & Petty, R. E. (1982). The need for cognition. *Journal of Personality and Social Psychology, 42*(1), 116–131.

Cauberghe, V., & De Pelsmacker, P. (2010). Advergames. *Journal of Advertising, 39*(1), 5–18. Retrieved from https://doi.org/10.2753/JOA0091-3367390101.

Charsky, D., & Mims, C. (2008). Integrating commercial off-the-shelf video games into school curriculums. *TechTrends, 52*(5), 38–44. Retrieved from https://doi.org/10. 1007/s11528-008-0195-0.

Connolly, T. M., Boyle, E., MacArthur, E., Hainey, T., & Boyle, J. M. (2012). A systematic literature review of empirical evidence on computer games and serious games. *Computers & Education, 59*(2), 661–686. Retrieved from https://doi.org/10.1016/j.compedu.2012. 03.004.

Coulson, M., & Ferguson, C. J. (2015). The influence of digital games on aggression and violent crime. In R. Kowert & T. Quandt (Eds.), *The video game debate* (pp. 54–73). New York: Routledge. Retrieved from https://doi.org/10.4324/9781315736495-4.

Crecente, D. (2014). Gaming against violence: A grassroots approach to teen dating violence. *Games for Health Journal, 3*(4), 198–201. Retrieved from https://doi.org/10. 1089/g4h.2014.0010.

Crutzen, R., van't Riet, J., & Short, C. E. (2015). Enjoyment: A conceptual exploration and overview of experimental evidence in the context of games for health. *Games for Health Journal, 5*(1), 15–20. Retrieved from https://doi.org/10.1089/g4h.2015.0059.

Daniels, J., & Lalone, N. (2012). Racism in video gaming: Connecting extremist and mainstream expressions of white supremacy. In D. Embrick & E. Lukacs (Eds.), *Social exclusion, power and video game play* (pp. 83–97). Lanham, Maryland: Lexington Press.

Dankbaar, M. E. W., Alsma, J., Jansen, E. E. H., van Merrienboer, J. J. G., van Saase, J. L. C. M., & Schuit, S. C. E. (2016a). An experimental study on the effects of a simulation game on students' clinical cognitive skills and motivation. *Advances in Health Sciences Education, 21*(3), 505–521. Retrieved from https://doi.org/10.1007/s10459-015-9641-x.

Dankbaar, M. E. W., Roozeboom, M. B., Oprins, E. A. P. B., Rutten, F., van Merrienboer, J. J. G., van Saase, J. L. C. M., & Schuit, S. C. E. (2016b). Preparing residents effectively in emergency skills training with a serious game. *Simulation in Healthcare: The Journal of the Society for Simulation in Healthcare, 12*(1), 9–16. Retrieved from https://doi.org/10.1097/SIH.0000000000000194.

Darrow, C. (1935). *Monopoly*. Parker Brothers.

De Grove, F., van Looy, J., Neys, J., & Jansz, J. (2012). Playing in school or at home? An exploration of the effects of context on educational game experience. *Electronic Journal of E-Learning, 10*(2), 199–208.

de la Hera Conde-Pumpido, T. (2015). A theoretical model for the study of persuasive communication through digital games. In J. M. Parreno, C. R. Mafe, & L. Scribner (Eds.), *Engaging consumers through branded entertainment and convergent media* (pp. 74–88). Hershey, PA: IGI Global. Retrieved from https://doi.org/10.4018/ 978-1-4666-8342-6.

de la Hera Conde-Pumpido, T. (2017). Persuasive gaming: Identifying the different types of persuasion through games. *International Journal of Serious Games*, *4*(1), 31–39. Retrieved from https://doi.org/10.17083/ijsg.v4i1.140.

de Smale, S., Kors, M. J. L., & Sandovar, A. M. (2019). The case of This war of mine: A production studies perspective on moral game design. *Games and Culture*, *14*(4), 387–409. Retrieved from https://doi.org/10.1177/1555412017725996.

DeSmet, A., van Ryckeghem, D., Compernolle, S., Baranowski, T., Thompson, D., Crombez, G., ... De Bourdeaudhuij, I. (2014). A meta-analysis of serious digital games for healthy lifestyle promotion. *Preventive Medicine*, *69*, 95–107. Retrieved from https://doi.org/10.1016/j.ypmed.2014.08.026.

Destructive Creations (2015). Hatred.[video game].

Devlin, S., Cowling, P. I., Kudenko, D., Goumagias, N., Nucciareli, A., Cabras, I., ... Feng Li. (2014). Game intelligence. In 2014 IEEE Conference on Computational Intelligence and Games (pp. 1–8). Dortmund, Germany: IEEE. Retrieved from https://doi.org/10.1109/CIG.2014.6932917.

Djaouti, D., Alvarez, J., Jessel, J.-P., & Rampnoux, O. (2011). Origins of serious games. In *Serious Games and edutainment applications* (pp. 25–43). London: Springer London. Retrieved from https://doi.org/10.1007/978-1-4471-2161-9_3.

Eindhoven University of Technology. (2015). *A breathtaking journey*. Eindhoven University of Technology.

Elson, M., Breuer, J., Ivory, J. D., & Quandt, T. (2014). More than stories with buttons: Narrative, mechanics, and context as determinants of player experience in digital games. *Journal of Communication*, *64*(3), 521–542. Retrieved from https://doi.org/10.1111/jcom.12096.

Erasmus University Medical Center, & IJsfontein. (2013). *abcdeSIM*. Erasmus University Medical Center.

Erb, U. (2015). Possibilities and limitations of transferring an educational simulation game to a digital platform. *Simulation & Gaming*, *46*(6), 817–837. Retrieved from https://doi.org/10.1177/1046878115621980.

Faber, T., Dankbaar, M., & van Merrienboer, J. (2018). Applying an instructional design method to serious games – Experiences and lessons learned. In 2018 9th International Conference on Information, Intelligence, Systems and Applications (IISA) (pp. 1–3). Larnaca, Cyprus: IEEE. Retrieved from https://doi.org/10.1109/IISA.2018.8633666.

Flanagan, M., & Nissenbaum, H. (2014). *Values at play in digital games*. Cambridge, Massachusetts: MIT Press.

Games4Change Europe.(2011). From serious games to games for impact. Retrieved from http://www.g4ceurope.eu/from-serious-games-to-games-for-impact/.

Garris, R., Ahlers, R., & Driskell, J. E. (2002). Games, motivation, and learning: A research and practice model. *Simulation & Gaming*, *33*(4), 441–467. https://doi.org/10.1177/1046878102238607.

Gerling, K. M., Mandryk, R. L., Birk, M. V., Miller, M., & Orji, R. (2014). The effects of embodied persuasive games on player attitudes toward people using wheelchairs. In Proceedings of the SIGCHI Conference on Human Factors in Computing Systems, 3413–3422. Retrieved from https://doi.org/10.1145/2556288.2556962.

Goris, J., Jalink, M. B., & ten Cate Hoedemaker, H. O. (2014). Training basic laparoscopic skills using a custom-made video game. *Perspectives on Medical Education*, *3*(4), 314–318. Retrieved from https://doi.org/10.1007/s40037-013-0106-8.

Granic, I., Lobel, A., & Engels, R. C. M. E. (2013). The benefits of playing video games. *American Psychologist*, *69*(1), 66–78. Retrieved from Retrieved from https://doi.org/10.1037/a0034857.

Grendel Games. (2015). Underground. Retrieved from https://grendelgames.com/game/underground/.

Haring, P., Chakinska, D., & Ritterfeld, U. (2011). Understanding serious gaming: A psychological perspective. In *Handbook of research on improving learning and motivation through educational games: Multidisciplinary approaches* (pp. 413–430). Dortmund, Germany: IGI Global. Retrieved from https://doi.org/10.4018/978-1-60960-495-0.ch020.

Heeter, C. (2009). Book review: Serious games: Mechanisms and effects. *International Journal of Gaming and Computer-Mediated Simulations*, *1*(3), 89–94.

Iacovides, I., & Cox, A. L. (2015). Moving beyond fun: Evaluating serious experience in digital games. In Proceedings of the 33rd Annual ACM Conference on Human Factors in Computing Systems – CHI '15 (pp. 2245–2254). New York, USA: ACM Press. Retrieved from https://doi.org/10.1145/2702123.2702204.

IJgosse, W. M., van Goor, H., & Luursema, J.-M. (2018). Saving robots improves laparoscopic performance: Transfer of skills from a serious game to a virtual reality simulator. *Surgical Endoscopy*, *32*(7), 3192–3199. Retrieved from https://doi.org/10.1007/s00464-018-6036-0.

iMinds. (2010). *Poverty Is Not A Game*. Retrieved July 14, 2014, from Retrieved from http://www.povertyisnotagame.com/?lang=en.

Iten, N., & Petko, D. (2016). Learning with serious games: Is fun playing the game a predictor of learning success? *British Journal of Educational Technology*, *47*(1), 151–163. Retrieved from https://doi.org/10.1111/bjet.12226.

Jacobs, R. S. (2017). *Playing to win over: Validating persuasive games*. Erasmus University Rotterdam. Retrieved from https://repub.eur.nl/pub/102769.

Jacobs, R. S. (2018). Play to win over: Effects of persuasive games. *Psychology of Popular Media Culture*, *7*(3), 231–240. Retrieved from https://doi.org/10.1037/ppm0000124.

Jacobs, R. S., Jansz, J., & de la Hera Conde-Pumpido, T. (2017). The key features of persuasive games: A model and case analysis. In R. Kowert & T. Quandt (Eds.), *New Perspectives on the Social Aspects of Digital Gaming: Multiplayer 2* (pp. 153–171). Oxford: Routledge.

Jacobs, R. S., Kneer, J., & Jansz, J. (2019). Playing against abuse: Effects of procedural and narrative persuasive games. *Journal of Games, Self, and Society*, *1*(1), 97–120. Retrieved from https://doi.org/10.1184/R1/7857578.

Jenkins, H., Camper, B., Chisholm, A., Grigsby, N., Klopfer, E., Osterweil, S., … Guan, T. C. (2009). From serious games to serious gaming. In U. Ritterfeld, M. Cody, & P. Vorderer (Eds.), *Serious games: Mechanisms and effects* (pp.448–468). New York/London: Routledge.

Jennifer Ann's Group. (2019). *Rispek Danis*. Retrieved from http://rispekdanis.com/.

Juul, J. (2013). *The art of failure: An essay on the pain of playing video games. Choice Reviews Online* (Vol. 51). Cambridge, MA: MIT Press. Retrieved from https://doi.org/10.5860/choice.51-1301.

Kato, P. M. (2012). Evaluating efficacy and validating games for health. *Games for Health Journal*, *1*(1), 74–76. Retrieved from https://doi.org/10.1089/g4h.2012.1017.

Kaufman, G., Flanagan, M., & Seidman, M. (2016). Creating stealth game interventions for attitude and behavior change: An "embedded design" model. *Transactions of the Digital Games Research Association*, *2*(3), 1–13. Retrieved from https://doi.org/10.26503/todigra.v2i3.57.

Kors, M. J. L., Ferri, G., van der Spek, E. D., Ketel, C., & Schouten, B. A. M. (2016). A Breathtaking Journey. On the design of an empathy-arousing mixed-reality game. In *Proceedings of the 2016 Annual Symposium on Computer-Human Interaction in Play – CHI PLAY '16* (pp. 91–104). New York, NY: ACM Press. https://doi.org/10.1145/2967934.2968110.

Landers, R. N. (2014). Developing a theory of gamified learning. *Simulation & Gaming*, 45(6), 752–768. Retrieved from https://doi.org/10.1177/1046878114563660.

Magie, E. (1904). *The Landlord's Game*.

Magnuson, J. (2011). *The Killer: A new notgame from Cambodia*. Retrieved from https://www.gametrekking.com/blog/the-killer-a-new-notgame-from-cambodia.

Malliet, S., Thysen, P., & Poels, K. (2011). Digital game rhetoric and critical reasoning: the case of "Grand Theft Auto IV" and "America's Army: Special Forces." In K. Poels & S. Malliet (Eds.), *Vice city virtue: Moral issues in digital game play* (pp. 245–265). Leuven: Acco Publishers.

Maxis. (1989). *SimCity*. Maxis.

McGonigal, J. (2011). *Reality is broken: Why games make us better and how they can change the world*. London: Penguin.

Metro Trains Melbourne. (2013). *Dumb Ways to Die*. Metro Trains Melbourne.

Michael, D. R., & Chen, S. L. (2005). *Serious games: Games that educate train, and inform*. New York: Muska & Lipman/Premier-Trade.

MicroProse. (1991). *Civilization*. MicroProse.

Mukherjee, S. (2016). Video games and slavery. *Transactions of the Digital Games Research Association*, 2(3), 243–257. Retrieved from https://doi.org/10.26503/todigra.v2i3.60.

Mulcahy, R. F., Russell-Bennett, R., Zainuddin, N., & Kuhn, K.-A. (2018). Designing gamified transformative and social marketing services. *Journal of Service Theory and Practice*, 28(1), 26–51. Retrieved from https://doi.org/10.1108/JSTP-02-2017-0034.

Neys, J., & Jansz, J. (2010). Political internet games: Engaging an audience. *European Journal of Communication*, 25(3), 227–241. Retrieved from https://doi.org/10.1177/0267323110373456.

Niantic. (2016). *Pokémon Go*. Niantic.

Nintendo. (2003). *WarioWare, Inc.: Mega Microgame$*. Nintendo.

Oliver, M. B., & Bartsch, A. (2010). Appreciation as audience response: Exploring entertainment gratifications beyond hedonism. *Human Communication Research*, 36(1), 53–81. Retrieved from https://doi.org/10.1111/j.1468-2958.2009.01368.x.

Overtoom, E. M., Jansen, F.-W., van Santbrink, E. J. P., Schraffordt Koops, S. E., Veersema, S., & Schreuder, H. W. R. (2017). Training in basic laparoscopic surgical skills: Residents' opinion of the new Nintendo Wii-U laparoscopic simulator. *Journal of Surgical Education*, 74(2), 352–359. Retrieved from https://doi.org/10.1016/j.jsurg.2016.10.004.

Peña, J., Hernández Pérez, J. F., Khan, S., & Cano Gómez, Á. P. (2018). Game perspective-taking effects on players' behavioral intention, attitudes, subjective norms, and self-efficacy to help immigrants: The case of "Papers, Please." *Cyberpsychology, Behavior, and Social Networking*, 21(11), 687–693. Retrieved from https://doi.org/10.1089/cyber.2018.0030.

Peng, W., Lee, M., & Heeter, C. (2010). The effects of a serious game on role-taking and willingness to help. *Journal of Communication*, 60(4), 723–742. Retrieved from https://doi.org/10.1111/j.1460-2466.2010.01511.x.

Petty, R. E., & Wegener, D. T. (1999). The elaboration likelihood model: Current status and controversies. In S. Chaiken & Y. Trope (Eds.), *Dual-process theories in social psychology* (pp. 37–72). New York: Guildford Press.

Pivik, J., McComas, J., Macfarlane, I., & Laflamme, M. (2002). Using virtual reality to teach disability awareness. *Journal of Educational Computing Research*, *26*(2), 203–218. Retrieved from https://doi.org/10.2190/WACX-1VR9-HCMJ-RTKB.

Pope, L. (2014). *The Sea Has No Claim*. Retrieved from https://dukope.com/sea/play.html.

Raphael, C., Bachen, C., Lynn, K. M., Baldwin-Philippi, J., & McKee, K. A. (2010). Games for civic learning: A conceptual framework and agenda for research and design. *Games and Culture*, *5*, 199–235.

Ratan, R., & Ritterfeld, U. (2009). Classifying serious games. In U. Ritterfeld, M. Cody, & P. Vorderer (Eds.), *Serious games: Mechanisms and effects*. New York/London: Routledge.

Rawlings, T. (2012). *My Cotton Picking Life*. Bristol, UK: GameTheNews. Retrieved from Retrieved from http://gamethenews.net/index.php/my-cotton-picking-life/.

Ritterfeld, U. (2009). Identity construction and emotion regulation in digital gaming. In U. Ritterfeld, M. Cody, & P. Vorderer (Eds.), *Serious games: Mechanisms and effects*. New York/London: Routledge.

Ruggiero, D. (2015). The effect of playing a persuasive game on attitude and affective learning. *Computers in Human Behavior*, *45*, 213–221. Retrieved from https://doi.org/10.1016/j.chb.2014.11.062.

Ruggiero, D., & Becker, K. (2015). Games you can't win. *The Computer Games Journal*, *4*(3–4), 169–186. Retrieved from https://doi.org/10.1007/s40869-015-0013-9.

Rüppel, U., & Schatz, K. (2011). Designing a BIM-based serious game for fire safety evacuation simulations. *Advanced Engineering Informatics*, *25*(4), 600–611. Retrieved from https://doi.org/10.1016/j.aei.2011.08.001.

Satava, R. M. (1993). Virtual reality surgical simulator. *Surgical Endoscopy*, *7*(3), 203–205. Retrieved from https://doi.org/10.1007/BF00594110.

Sherry, J. L. (2015). Debating how to learn from video games. In R. Kowert & T. Quandt (Eds.), *The video game debate* (pp. 116–130). New York: Routledge.

Šisler, V. (2016). Contested memories of war in *Czechoslovakia 38–39: Assassination*: Designing a serious game on contemporary history. *Game Studies*, *16*(2). Retrieved from Retrieved from http://gamestudies.org/1602/articles/sisler.

Six to Start. (2012). *Zombies, Run!* Six to Start.

Slater, M. D. (2002). Entertainment education and the persuasive impact of narratives. In M. C. Green, J. J. Strange, & T. C. Brock (Eds.), *Narrative impact: Social and cognitive foundations* (pp. 157–181). New York/Hove:Psychology Press.

Soflano, M. (2011). Modding in serious games: Teaching structured query language (SQL) using *NeverWinter Nights*. In M. Ma, A. Oikonomou, & L. Jain (Eds.), *Serious games and edutainment applications* (pp. 347–368). London: Springer. Retrieved from https://doi.org/10.1007/978-1-4471-2161-9_18.

Spagnolli, A., Chittaro, L., & Gamberini, L. (2016). Interactive persuasive systems: a perspective on theory and evaluation. *International Journal of Human-Computer Interaction*, *32*(3), 177–189. Retrieved from https://doi.org/10.1080/10447318.2016.1142798.

Steinemann, S. T., Iten, G. H., Opwis, K., Forde, S. F., Frasseck, L., & Mekler, E. D. (2017). Interactive narratives affecting social change: A closer look at the relationship between interactivity and prosocial behavior. *Journal of Media Psychology*, *29*(1), 54–66. Retrieved from https://doi.org/10.1027/1864-1105/a000211.

Sterczewski, P. (2016). This uprising of mine: Game conventions, cultural memory and civilian experience of war in Polish games. *Game Studies, 16*(2). Retrieved from http://gamestudies.org/1602/articles/sterczewski.

Stieler-Hunt, C. J., & Jones, C. M. (2017). Feeling alienated – Teachers using immersive digital games in classrooms. *Technology, Pedagogy and Education, 26*(4), 457–470. Retrieved from https://doi.org/10.1080/1475939X.2017.1334227.

Treanor, M., & Mateas, M. (2009). Newsgames: Procedural rhetoric meets political cartoons. *Breaking New Ground: Innovation in Games, Play, Practice and Theory – Proceedings of DiGRA 2009.* Retrieved from http://coolvideogames.org/goto/http://www.wingchunsantacruz.com/gamesandart/research/newsgames-DiGRA2009.pdf.

United States Army. (2002). *America's Army.* United States Army.

Van Oostendorp, H., Warmelink, H., & Jacobs, R. S. (2016). *The evaluation of health-oriented serious games and apps: A differentiated approach.* Retrieved from https://www.dutchgamegarden.nl/growing-games-presents-the-validation-research-report/.

Vidani, A. C., Chittaro, L., & Carchietti, E. (2010). Assessing nurses' acceptance of a serious game for emergency medical services. In *2nd International Conference on Games and Virtual Worlds for Serious Applications, VS-GAMES 2010* (pp. 101–108). Larnaca, Cyprus: IEEE. Retrieved from https://doi.org/10.1109/VS-GAMES.2010.12.

Vyvey, T., Núñez Castellar, E. P., & Van Looy, J. (2018). Loaded with fun? the impact of enjoyment and cognitive load on brand retention in digital games. *Journal of Interactive Advertising, 18*(1), 72–82. Retrieved from https://doi.org/10.1080/15252019.2018.1446370.

Waiguny, M. K. J., Nelson, M. R., & Marko, B. (2013). How advergame content influences explicit and implicit brand attitudes: When violence spills over. *Journal of Advertising, 42*(2–3), 155–169. Retrieved from https://doi.org/10.1080/00913367.2013.774590.

Witkowski, E. (2013). Running from zombies. In *Proceedings of the 9th Australasian Conference on Interactive Entertainment Matters of Life and Death – IE '13* (pp. 1–8). New York, New York, USA: ACM Press. Retrieved from https://doi.org/10.1145/2513002.2513573.

Woo, J. C. (2014). Digital game-based learning supports student motivation, cognitive success, and performance outcomes. *Educational Technology and Society, 17*(3), 291–307.

Wouters, P., van der Spek, E. D., & van Oostendorp, H. (2009). Current practices in serious game research. In *Games-based learning advancements for multi-sensory human computer interfaces* (pp. 232–250). Dortmund, Germany: IGI Global. Retrieved from https://doi.org/10.4018/978-1-60566-360-9.ch014.

Yager Development. (2012). *Spec Ops: The Line.* 2k Games.

4

DIGITAL DIVIDES AND STRUCTURAL INEQUALITIES

Exploring the Technomasculine Culture of Gaming

Thomas H. Apperley and Kishonna L. Gray

This chapter builds on prior work on the discrimination and inequalities that characterize digital game cultures, drawing on work from cultural studies, critical race scholarship, and feminism. It focuses on how the dominant default able-bodied, anglophone, cis-het, white technomasculine culture of gaming shapes the gaming experiences of people who do not conform to the hegemonic norms that culture has established. The chapter illustrates the historical impact of technomasculinity on inequality and discrimination in the diffusion of gaming technology through a discussion of the how early adopters of Microsoft Xbox Live services impacted the experiences of Black users. The wider influence of technomasculinity on online and gaming cultures is further elaborated through the #gamergate controversy. Finally, the chapter considers how the tactical responses from marginalized communities continue to challenge the hegemonic techno-masculinity of gaming culture. This chapter argues that an examination of inequality in digital play demonstrates the need to shift the dialogue around digital inequality beyond simply "access" to more nuanced understanding of the various matrices of exclusion that people deal with when using gaming technologies.

Introduction

The forms that discrimination and inequality take in gaming cultures are highly nuanced. Understanding how discrimination and inequality shape the experience of gamers who visibly differ from the dominant able-bodied, anglophone, cis-het, white "technomasculine" culture of gaming is crucial given the increasing emphasis on gaming in education and training and the ongoing integration of game-like elements into everyday processes through gamefication and gameful design. We recognize these differences create many ways for people to identify as both insiders and outsiders to gamer culture and perhaps to be marked as outsiders in multiple ways that exacerbate their experience of inequality. A further complication is that many who have bodies that do not conform to the dominant technomasculine gamer culture are nominally included in gaming cultures, but this inclusion requires a tacit agreement with the status quo, which effectively silences dissent (Salter & Blodgett, 2012). In this chapter, we draw on perspectives from cultural studies, critical race scholarship, and feminism to highlight the various exclusionary practices within gaming communities.

Despite a widespread perception that games and game-like activities permeate everyday life and mundane activities through the "ludefication of culture" (Raessens, 2006), this cultural change is experienced unevenly. While most people have basic access to gaming technologies, there are inequitable distributions in how users engage games, participate in gaming and esports communities, and perceive their participation in gaming contexts (Apperley, 2010; DiSalvo, Crowley, and Norwood 2008; Schott & Horrell, 2000). In the processes of becoming ingrained and embedded in our everyday social infrastructure, these inequalities in gaming often exacerbate existing inequalities, making it increasingly difficult for equitable participation. Furthermore, in some cases these inequalities have a role in sustaining cultures of hatred and hostility, where privilege is naturalized and gaming and networked gaming seen as technomasculine activities. As a consequence, women, people of color, disabled, queer, and gender nonconforming gamers are intruders into this space.

We explore the structural factors influencing inequality of usage of digital games through concept of "digital inequality" (DiMaggio et al., 2001, 2004) in usage. In applying this concept, we will explore what Hargittai (2001) has termed the "second level digital divide," which explores differences in internet use and the implications for the reproduction of social inequality (see also Hargittai & Hinnant, 2008; Hargittai, 2008). The "second level digital divide" in gaming occurs in a wide variety of contexts with remarkably different qualities that are also shaped by gender, sexuality, race, disability, and other economic factors. Often the focus is on *access*, but access provides no understanding of how technology is actually *used in practice* (Hargittai & Hinnant, 2008). It is crucial to move beyond the binary classification of "haves" and "have nots" and engage a more nuanced conceptualization of how people use technology (Barzilai-Nahon, 2006; DiMaggio & Hargittai, 2001; DiMaggio et al., 2004). In order to explore how structural inequality shapes the experiences of marginalized groups in gaming, in this chapter we first outline the historic role that white men and boys have had as the primary audience of digital games and the role their role as early adopters of gaming technologies has had in creating a technomasculine gaming culture. Next, we turn to explore the crucial role of symbolic violence in sustaining technomasculine dominance in gaming cultures. Finally, we consider how women; gender nonconforming; lesbian, gay, bisexual, trans, queer/questioning, intersex; people of color (LGBTIQ+); and disabled gamers have found niches for themselves within and against the dominant technomasculine gaming culture.

Inequitable Diffusion of Gaming Technologies

Gaming industries have succeeded in making digital games a mainstream form of everyday entertainment. Decades of commercial expansion have required the successful growth and maintenance of their user base and the continuous repositioning of gaming technologies at the cutting edge of domestic media technology. The rates of engaging with and adopting technologies are largely influenced by social and economic status, so with rapidly developing dynamic technologies, a "default user" is factored into the design and marketing of the technology. The gaming industry in North America and Europe has historically assigned White men as its target demographic (Paul, 2012). Dramatic changes that have occurred over the years about how the target audience of gaming is understood, primarily the economic significance of the casual and mobile gaming sector, led to a new recognition of the importance of women for the industry (Anable, 2018; Chess, 2017; Hjorth & Richardson, 2014). While these changes are welcome, they do not significantly impact the gaming experiences many excluded groups.

How the game industry acknowledges, understands, and encourages diversity among its users can also entrench and exacerbate existing inequalities. Within console gaming – in particular – male, female, trans-, and gender nonconforming identifying users of color have felt left behind by the dramatic changes incurred by the rapidly updating vision of the gaming audience, which, while more gender inclusive, is still predominantly understood as white (). For example, among the users of the Xbox One, Microsoft is considered to have been diligent about adhering to the changing needs of its user base. However, most changes reflect what is desirable for the majority of Xbox Live users, and given the number of users, it is unrealistic to assume that they all will be accommodated. This model of change and inclusion that values "listening" to the audience and audience engagement can end up valuing and privileging a "majority" position, which is often, in the case of Microsoft Xbox One, predominantly white. Marginalized users, particularly people of color, are unable to participate in the changing "face" of gaming because their individual voices are drowned out by the White majority.

The difficulties faced by marginalized users who wish to continue to eng in the changing conceptions of gaming technologies like the Xbox Or palpably illustrated in the widely used concept of "adopter categories" (

technologies. Adopter categories originate in Rogers' diffusion of innovation framework (Rogers, 1962); there are five categories – Innovators, Early Adopters, Early Majority, Late Majority, and Laggards – of which the first two are particularly relevant. "Innovators" are the first individuals to adopt a new technology; they are typically people that are willing to take risks, tend to be the youngest, have the highest social class, have great financial lucidity, are very social, and have the closest contact to scientific sources and interactions with other innovators. The second group, the "Early Adopters," tend to be younger, have a higher social status, more financial fluidity, advanced education, and are more socially forward than other people who eventually adopt the technology. These individuals interact regularly with Innovators and they rely on them to inform them about new innovations. There is not a huge difference between these two types. The Innovators often inform the Early Adopters on what to do and how to navigate the space – leading them both to adopt the innovation rather simultaneously. It is imperative to note that the majority of the individuals who are Innovators and Early Adopters in gaming also have enough recreational time and capital to devote to social and technological changes in gaming. What previous scholarship on the adopter categories has revealed is that the ways that White men are targeted and cultivated into becoming early adopters of gaming technologies (Lamb et al., 2009, p. 310). Such processes ensure ongoing dominance of technomasculine culture in gaming and make it difficult for people of color and other marginalized folk to shape the cultures of gaming by being early adopters.

One way that adaptor categories targeting white gamers exacerbate existing inequalities is illustrated in the privileging of the use of Standard American English in Xbox Live chats. While this may have seemed "natural" at some point in the history of the Xbox because the early adopters of the Xbox were primarily White men, now it acts to exclude already marginalized gamers from non-English speaking backgrounds and those identified as having Asian, Black, or Latino voices. The use of Standard American English impacts how information is disseminated in these spaces, creating a game culture that privileges those using or adopting it (Gray 2020, 2014). As this cultural privileging of voice continues, it also shapes the technical integration of voice into gaming software in networked games and how voice is embedded in the interface of the platform itself through voice activation. Thus, the cultural dominance of Standard American English has profound impact on new adopters of the Xbox One, who may have to spend considerable time training the console to "hear" their voice.

The cultivation of a White male audience for gaming has deep historic roots, which are tied to changing notions of masculinity. In her book *Coin-Operated Americans: Rebooting Boyhood at the Video Game Arcade*, Carly A. Kocurek (2015) provides a genealogical history of how video game arcades provided communities where masculinity and maleness were the two pillars that upheld them and how these trends exist and operate in contemporary game cultures. Kocurek asserts:

[G]ender inequalities in video gaming did not develop during the industry's postcrash resurrection or with the rise of home consoles; rather, these historical inequalities emerged through public discourse and public practice that accompanied the rise of video gaming's early commercial success in the coin-op industry (2015, p. xvi).

What is crucial about this stipulation is the notion that game cultures and the act of gaming itself have not always historically been considered a predominantly "male" one. Rather, through a variety of marketing strategies, the game industry has historically cultivated the relationship between masculinity and gaming in an attempt to make the experience of gaming seem elusive, exclusive, and special. To this end, Kocurek also considers the economic impact of the arcade, thereby connecting boyhood, capitalism, and public video gaming. She considers the construction of gaming spaces as masculine via this public discourse; by tracing this discursive history, she illustrates how in the decades of the 70s and 80s, video game arcades provided a means for a fledgling notion of technologically em-powered masculinity to thrive in the United States. This cemented the notion that gaming was an activity that was to be performed mostly by white, middle class boys and men (2015, p. 51).

Masculinity, Technoculture, and Violence

The intricate connections between masculinity and violence make it essential to discuss the means through which technomasculine gaming culture sustains in-equitable practices. Scholars of masculinity have noted that in the U.S. context, the dominant masculinity is hypermasculine and violent (Kimmel, 1997; Wesley, 2003). Kimmel argues that U.S. hypermasculinity is based on racism, sexism, and homophobia and marked by violent rapaciousness (1997, pp. 191–192). Wesley points out that as of 1978 "the United States was, without even a close contender, the most violent industrialized nation in the world" (2003, p. 1). This violence stems from deeply embedded cultural ideologies that privilege the sword over the pen, brute strength over intellect, and men over women. The rise of the gaming industry in the United States occurred around the same time as the peak violence identified by Wesley (2003). However, geek masculinity is often excluded from critiques of hypermasculinity (see Massanari, 2015), but the violent and materi-alistic identities and behaviors that constitute that constitute the dominant techno-masculine gaming culture share a great many qualities with the hypermasculinity earmarked by Kimmel that need to be further explored.

The growing technology sector of Silicon Valley represent the new centrality of this once hidden, often marginalized masculinities in U.S. culture and politics. According to Johnson, the technomasculinity of Silicon Valley can be defined as "an expression of masculinity that is oriented toward the mastery of technology and skilled use of technological tools and systems" (2018, n.p.). Johnson (2018) further suggests that this type of masculinity is often associated with individuals who are highly competent with computers but typically lacking in social or physical skills. Scholars have increasingly illustrated the ways that technomasculinity situates women and other non-masculine presenting folks as inferior. Such attitudes are illustrated in the memo written by Damore, 2017, who was critical of Google's commitments to diversity (namely increasing the role of women). It is necessary to explore these practices as exclusionary cultures. While direct violence does not constitute the bulk of the violence experienced by those marginalized by masculinity in gaming, it is important to understand that deliberate exclusion and implicit exclusion can be considered continuations of this violence. In sociology and cultural studies, this is often described as symbolic violence (Bourdieu & Wacquant, 1992), and the term is useful in this context as it provides us with a more nuanced way to make sense of how hypermasculine forms of violence are continued in the cultures of gaming through symbolic violence enacted through technomasculinity that has created a range of impactful exclusionary activities.

While feminists remain concerned with the continued negative representations of women in media, attention has also been given to the relationship between mediated representations and the experiences of women in physical settings, at least the manifestation of "real world" inequalities in digital settings. The same is true for video games. An illustrative example presents itself with the work of Salter and Blodgett (2012), which examines women existing within hypermasculinity in gaming publics (pre-#gamergate); as such, online gaming communities have been structured as "boy's clubs" that exclude women and non-gender-conforming individuals. From their observations of a webcomic series, Salter and Blodgett (2012) identify three archetypal roles that women are given to play within hardcore gaming circles: women as sex objects, women as invisible, and women as the enemy. These gendered roles are seen in other social institutions as well. Even more damaging, women who speak out for themselves are belittled, verbally assaulted, and harassed from inside and outside these gaming publics (Fox & Tang, 2014; Gray, 2012; Norris, 2004).

Some of the women and non-gender-conforming people who have experienced direct, indirect, and symbolic violence and threats of violence include Zoey Quinn, Brianna Wu, Felicia Day, and Anita Sarkeesian. Many of these threats have caused them to leave their homes for their own safety and to cancel public events and appearances, fearing for their lives (Rott, 2014). Sarkeesian's story in particular is one that is worth explicating in terms of the violence incurred by the proponents of the #gamergate controversy because negative responses to Sarkeesian's critiques of video games embodied the very tropes she discusses in her YouTube series, "Tropes vs. Women in Games" (Feminist Frequency., 2013–2015). This crowdfunded series explores the archetypal ways in which female characters have been portrayed in many popular games. This series draws heavily upon feminist critical theory and provides viewers with, as Sarkeesian states at the beginning of each video, the ability to enjoy games while still being critical of the content.

One of the more prominent points of Sarkeesian's series is that women are depicted in certain highly clichéd, gendered, and stereotypical ways in games (Feminist Frequency., 2013–2015). Women in games are often objects to look at and objectify, as opposed to their male counterparts, who are often more fully developed and well-rounded characters. In her videos, she takes great care to highlight the many ways in which female non-player characters are oftentimes violently disposed of, or treated, in games. Indeed, these methods range from the "Euthanized Damsel" (a damsel in distress who is killed by the player for her "own good") to women who are simply background decoration that players may dispose of at their whims. As entertainment experiences, video games have themselves historically employed violence as a rhetorical tool to advance plots and engage users in the often simplistic, conflict-driven in-game narrative. As Sarkeesian has pointed out, with a shocking regularity these violent narratives focus on women as continual victims, unable to defend themselves or even seek protection, while the player is positioned as a white masculine savior figure (Salter & Blodgett, 2017). Since posting, Sarkeesian has disabled commentary for each video that she has posted, in an attempt to stem the influx of hate mail and violent threats that she has received since posting her videos (Parkin, 2014). Theorizing gaming culture from this perspective, it is clear that the symbolic and real violence surrounding #gamergate revolves around sexist ideologies within the community that reflect society in general yet are somehow unconstrained, if not actually pandered to, by the industry.

Other aspects of gaming culture that act to embed this form of techno-masculine domination include various playstyles as well as the marketing and promotion of games and esports. For example, more casual players, including those who are new to video games or less comfortable with the controls, appear to engage in violent gameplay less often compared to their more experienced counterparts (Ribbens & Malliet, 2015). While solitary gamers may show an increase in aggression after playing violent video games, this effect dissolves when gamers play cooperatively with others (Velez et al., 2016). In fact, Velez Greitemeyer Whitaker Ewoldsen and Bushman (2016) found that participants who played cooperatively had similar levels of aggression to participants who did not play violent video games, suggesting a near zero increase in violent outcomes regardless of exposure to violent video games provided there was also social contact with others. But when factoring gender in experiences in interactions around gaming, the kinds of hostility and aggression women experience cannot be ignored, and the symbolic violence directed at women in game culture demands further research. The tendency to use hypersexualized women in videogame and esports marketing and advertising practices has also been well documented (see Taylor et al., 2009). This level of oppression and marginalization speaks to the symbolic nature of relegating women to social margins within video games and gaming culture.

The industry, games, and players all play a role in the attempts to subordinate women, whether overtly or covertly, limiting female gamers' agency and visibility while maintaining a hegemonic male order. The events of #gamergate were a cultural reaction to reassert the dominant technomasculine power over the subordinate group (women) as the sexism and gendered expectations within the gaming community rose to the surface and were revealed for critical analysis and assessment. We consider real and symbolic violence against women to be normalized such that its victims are expected to endure it and are punished when these expectations are broken (Gray, 2014). In this context, the dominant group, White male gamers, retain a vast majority of the power in video gaming culture (Gray, 2014). This domination is sustained by the gaming industry by continually marketing to and catering to this demographic (Gray, 2012), at the cost of the exclusion of others. This level of subordination has led to significant threats of violence digitally and physically. Because of the normalization of this culture within gaming, it is necessary to examine the process that leads to this reality, and symbolic violence is useful in understanding this trend. And while no narrative within gaming is fixed, the use of violence as a means to propel a narrative has been molded for generations and rooted in a culture that continues to situate violence as normal.

Challenging Exclusion and Discrimination

Many of the cultures of users on the peripheries of technomasculine gaming culture are "making do" with otherwise ignored, outmoded, and marginalized technologies or practices that can build and sustain communities that challenge the reproduction of inequality. The differential uses of gaming technologies by marginalized users must also be recognized for their potential to lead to increasingly transformative ways of participation. Harvey (2014), for example, highlights the innovative game design taking place with the Twine platform, which has also provided scope for many people outside of the technomasculine demographic to gain experience in game design (cf. Anthropy, 2012). Research conducted on gameplay practices in a Venezuelan cybercafé indicated that game piracy was crucial for video game play to occur in that context (Apperley, 2010, 2019), suggesting that the innovative digital rights management regimes of the last decade enforce an ongoing unevenness between the global "north" and "south." The experience gap between players in developing countries and what is generally understood to be "normal" is further examined by Phillip Penix-Tadsen (2016, 2019), who explores, among other themes, the role of unlicensed localization of games in building local games industries in the countries of the global south.

Similarly, female gamers have also found various methods to counteract gendered oppression (Cote, 2017; Gray, 2013). One such method is griefing, which is when an individual or group intentionally plays in a manner unintended by the game developers to make the game less enjoyable for others (Gray, 2014). This method is often used to resist domination from sexist comments or attacks against female players and is particularly effective when utilized by a group of women. As they disrupt the comfortableness of the technomasculine dominant gamers by "ruining" their fun, such tactics are similar to those of the "feminist spoilsport," a reimagining of Sara Ahmed's (2017) "feminist killjoy" for gaming cultures (Boluk & LeMieux, 2017).

Other marginalized groups have used similar tactics that blend disruptive in-game practices with consumer-based demands. Resistance tactics include boycotting particular games; using gaming services to file complaints against players; and posting to social media, gaming websites, and discussion boards (Gray, 2014). Furthermore, in-game protests from marginalized groups that are aimed at disrupting play and attracting the attention of the corporate owners of the game have a long history in networked gaming; they have occurred in *Ultima Online, EverQuest, City of Heroes, Westward Journey,* and *Star Wars Galaxies* (Apperley, 2010; Chan, 2009). Although sometimes these activities are aimed at simply reforming the rules of the game, they are often driven by a nominal notion of fairness that is shaped by technomasculine assumptions that games make everyone equal. However, some in-game protest movements were more concerned with the inclusivity of the games themselves; for example, protests were made in *World of Warcraft* after Blizzard had threatened to expel players that were promoting their guild as "gay-friendly" from the game (Ward, 2006). These forms of protest, while often involving issues that parallel offline political concerns, challenge the authority of the owners and managers of the games and game communities to make decisions that impact the players' experiences by bringing the "real" world into play. Protesting against authorities highlights the arbitrary construction of the virtual and can elevate the stakes of play by establishing resonances between injustices in the games and those that take place in everyday life (Apperley, 2010, p. 113).

Conclusion

Gaming cultures serve as an ongoing example of how media continue to be significant sites where exaggerated forms of hypermasculinity are performed. Gender "provides a way to decode meaning and to understand the complex connections among various forms of human interactions" (Scott, 1986, p. 1067). The coding of masculinity establishes a gendered hierarchy of power, especially in the myriad ways that masculinity is depicted. This masculine hierarchy is prominent and visible within gaming. But women and other marginalized folks continue to resist and highlight their own experiences to establish a plurality of gaming cultures.

What is understood to be at stake in videogame play has changed in time since the videogame industry began cultivating a masculine image. The connection that games have with civics and communities and the growing connection between digital gaming and new forms of cultural expression on communicative platforms like *Twitch* indicate how digital play can shift the dialogue around digital inequality beyond access. The kinds of knowledge, skills, and literacies cultivated through play and inclusion in game cultures suggest not just access to nascent communicative forms but also a global participatory culture. Digital play and digital games are an access point to more than just entertainment: they must also be understood as technologies that can cultivate and produce equal opportunities just as much as they can embed discriminatory practices.

Acknowledgments

Thomas H. Apperley's contribution to this work was enabled by the Academy of Finland funded Centre of Excellence in Game Culture Studies [grant number 312395].

References

Ahmed, S. (2017). *Living a feminist life*. Durham, NC: Duke University Press.

Anable, A. (2018). *Playing with feelings: Video games and affect*. Minneapolis: University of Minnesota Press.

Anthropy, A. (2012). *Rise of the videogame zinesters: How freaks, normals, amateurs, artists, dreamers, drop-outs, queers, housewives, and people like you are taking back an art form*. New York, NY: Seven Stories Press.

Apperley, T. (2010). *Gaming rhythms: Play and counterplay from the situated to the global*. Amsterdam, Netherlands: Institute of Network Cultures.

Apperley, T. (2019). Digital gaming's South-South connection. In P. Penix-Tadsen (Ed.), *Videogames in the global south* (pp. 211–221). Pittsburgh, PA: ETC Press.

Barzilai-Nahon, K. (2006). Gaps and bits: Conceptualizing measurements for digital divide/s. *The Information Society, 22*(5), 269–278.

Boluk, S., & LeMieux, P. (2017). *Metagaming: Playing, competing, spectating, cheating, trading, making, and breaking videogames*. Minneapolis: University of Minnesota Press.

Bourdieu, P., & Wacquant, L. J. (1992). *An invitation to reflexive sociology*. Chicago, IL: University of Chicago Press.

Chan, D. (2009). Beyond the "Great Fire-Wall": The case of in-game protests in China. L. Hjorth & D. Chan (Eds.), *Gaming cultures and place in the Asia-Pacific* (pp. 141–157). London, UK: Routledge.

Chess, S. (2017). *Ready player two: Women gamers and designed identity*. Minneapolis: University of Minnesota Press.

Cote, A. (2017). "I Can Defend Myself": Women's strategies for coping with harassment while gaming online. *Games & Culture, 12*(2), 136–155. 10.1177/1555412015587603.

Damore, J. (2017). Google's ideological echo chamber. Retrieved from https://assets.documentcloud.org/documents/3914586/Googles-Ideological-Echo-Chamber.pdf.

DiMaggio, P., & Hargittai, E. (2001). *From the "digital divide" to "digital inequality": Studying internet use as penetration increases*. Princeton: Centre for Arts and Cultural Policy Studies, Woodrow Wilson School, Princeton University, 4(1), 2–4.

DiMaggio, P., Hargittai, E., Celeste, C., & Shafer, S. (2004). Digital inequality: From unequal access to differentiated use. In *Social inequality* (pp. 355–400). Russell Sage Foundation.

DiSalvo, B. J., Crowley, K., & Norwood, R. (2008). Learning in context: Digital games and young Black men. *Games & Culture, 3*(2), 131–141. doi: 10.1177/1555412008314130.

Feminist Frequency. (2013–2015). *Tropes vs women in videogames—Season one* [video playlist]. YouTube. Retrieved from https://www.youtube.com/playlist?list=PLn4ob_5_ttEaA_vc8F3fjzE62esf9yP61.

Fox, J., & Tang, W. Y. (2014). Sexism in online video games: The role of conformity to masculine norms and social dominance orientation. *Computers in Human Behavior, 33*, 314–320. doi: 10.1016/j.chb.2013.07.014.

Gray, K. L. (2012). Deviant bodies, stigmatized identities, and racist acts: Examining the experiences of African-American gamers in Xbox Live. *New Review of Hypermedia and Multimedia, 18*(4), 261–276. doi: 10.1080/13614568.2012.746740.

Gray, K. L. (2013). Collective organizing, individual resistance, or asshole griefers? An ethnographic analysis of women of color in Xbox Live. *Ada: A Journal of Gender, New Media, and Technology, 2*. Retrieved from https://adanewmedia.org/2013/06/issue2-gray/.

Gray, K. L. (2014). *Race, gender, and deviance in Xbox Live: Theoretical perspectives from the virtual margins*. New York, NY: Routledge.

Gray, K. L. (2020) Intersectional tech: The transmediated experiences of Black users in digital gaming. Baton Rouge, LA: LSU Press.

Hargittai, E. (2001). Second-level digital divide: Mapping differences in people's online skills. *First Monday, 7*(4). arXivpreprintcs/0109068.

Hargittai, E. (2008). The role of expertise in navigating links of influence. In J. Turow & L. Tsui (Eds.), *The hyperlinked society: Questioning connections in the digital age* (pp. 85–103). Ann Arbor: University of Michigan Press.

Hargittai, E., & Hinnant, A. (2008). Digital inequality: Differences in young adults' use of the internet. *Communication Research, 35*(5), 602–621. doi: 10.1177/0093650208321782.

Harvey, A. (2014). Twine's revolution: Democratization, depoliticization, and the queering of game design. *GAME: The Italian Journal of Game Studies, 3*, 95–107. Retrieved from https://www.gamejournal.it/3_harvey/.

Hjorth, L., & Richardson, I. (2014). *Gaming in social, locative and mobile media*. London, UK: Palgrave.

Johnson, R. (2018). Technomasculinity and its influence in video game production. In N. Taylor & G. Voorhees (Eds.), *Masculinities in play* (pp. 249–262). London, UK: Palgrave. doi: 10.1007/978-3-319-90581-5_14.

Kimmel, M. S. (1997). Masculinity as homophobia: Fear, shame and silence in the construction of gender identity. In M. M. Gergen & S. N. Davis (Eds.), *Toward a new psychology of gender* (pp. 223–242). New York, NY: Routledge.

Kocurek, C. A. (2015). *Coin-operated Americans: Rebooting boyhood at the video game arcade*. Minneapolis: University of Minnesota Press.

Lamb, C. W., Hair, J. H., & McDaniel, C. D. (2009). *Essentials of marketing 6th ed*. Mason (Ohio): South-Western.

Massanari, A. (2015). *Participatory Culture, Community, and Play: Learning from Reddit*. New York, NY: Peter Lang.

Norris, K. (2004). Gender stereotypes, aggression, and computer games: An online survey of women. *CyberPsychology & Behavior, 7*(6), 714–727. doi: 10.1089/cpb.2004.7.714.

Parkin, S. (2014, October 17). Gamergate: A scandal erupts in the video-game community. *The New Yorker*. Retrieved from https://www.newyorker.com/tech/annals-of-technology/gamergate-scandal-erupts-video-game-community.

Paul, C. (2012). *Wordplay and the discourse of video games: Analyzing words, design, and play*. New York, NY: Routledge.

Penix-Tadsen, P. (2016). *Cultural vode: Videogames and Latin America.* Cambridge, MA: MIT Press.

Penix-Tadsen, P. (2019). Introduction. In P. Penix-Tadsen (Ed.), *Video games and the global south* (pp. 1–32). Pittsburgh, PA: ETC Press.

Raessens, J. (2006). Playful identities, or the ludification of culture. *Games & Culture, 1*(1), 52–57. doi: 10.1177/1555412005281779.

Ribbens, W., & Malliet, S. (2015). How male young adults construe their playing style in violent video games. *New Media & Society, 17*(10), 1624–1642. doi: 10.1177/1461444814530821.

Rott, N. (2014, September 24). #Gamergate controversy fuels debate on women and video games. National Public Radio. Retrieved from https://www.npr.org/sections/alltechconsidered/2014/09/24/349835297/-gamergate-controversy-fuels-debate-on-women-and-video-games?t=1585555937988.

Rogers, E. M. (1962). *Diffusion of innovations* (1st ed.). New York, NY: Free Press of Glencoe.

Salter, A., & Blodgett, B. (2012). Hypermasculinity & Dickwolves: The contentious role of women in the new gaming public. *Journal of Broadcasting & Electronic Media, 56*(3), 401–416. doi: 10.1080/08838151.2012.705199.

Salter, A., & Blodgett, B. (2017). *Toxic geek masculinity in media: Sexism, trolling, and identity policing.* New York, NY: Palgrave.

Schott, G. R., & Horrell, K. R. (2000). Girl gamers and their relationship with the gaming culture. *Convergence, 6*(4), 36–53. doi: 10.1177/135485650000600404.

Scott, J. W. (1986). Gender: A useful category of historical analysis. *The American Historical Review, 91*(5), 1053–1075. doi: 10.2307/1864376.

Taylor, N., Jenson, J., & de Castell, S. (2009). Cheerleaders/booth babes/ Halo hoes: Pro-gaming, gender and jobs for the boys. *Digital Creativity, 20*(4), 239–252. doi: 10.1080/14626260903290323.

Ward, M. (2006, February 13). Gay rights win in Warcraft world. BBC News. Retrieved from http://news.bbc.co.uk/2/hi/technology/4700754.stm.

Wesley, M. C. (2003). *Violent adventure.* Charlottesville: Virginia University Press.

Velez, J., Greitemeyer, T., Whitaker, J. L., Ewoldsen, D. R., & Bushman, B. J. (2016). Violent video games and reciprocity: The attenuating effects of cooperative game play on subsequent aggression. *Communications Research, 43*(4), 447–467. doi: 10.1177/0093650214552519.

5

TWITCH AND PARTICIPATORY CULTURES

Ashley M.L. Brown and Lis Moberly

Why watch someone else play videogames when you could just play them yourself? This chapter answers this common question while using the popular streaming platform Twitch.tv to debate the notion that videogames are antisocial activities and that watching gameplay is an inactive form of media consumption. This chapter argues that streaming platforms such as Twitch afford a different flavor of interactivity, but interactivity nonetheless. Instead of interacting with a game, viewers are interacting real-time with a live streamer and a community of other viewers while still absorbing the content of a game. The chapter includes three sections: The Rise of the Streamer (how individuals with webcams became celebrities), Twitch and Gaming Communities (the role of Twitch in developing and sustaining gaming communities), and Equal Participation (a brief discussion of disparities in their popularity based on gender and race). The focus of this chapter is to dispel some common misconceptions about the uses and effects of this medium and provide insight into what Twitch is, what it isn't, and what it may be in the future.

Introduction

Although there are many streaming websites, like YouTube and Mixer, that allow people to broadcast themselves and watch livestreams in real time, Twitch (www.twitch.tv) is arguably the go-to website for videogame streaming. The site is perhaps most known for its role in popularizing and making competitive e-sports widely accessible (Taylor, 2012; Witkowski, 2012). Although e-sports might be how Twitch became famous (for a more in-depth discussion of e-sports, see Chapter 8 in this volume), not every channel features competitive gaming or even digital games at all. In fact, recently Twitch has made efforts to make its IRL (in real life; where individuals showcase real-life talents and hobbies such as cooking and do-it-yourself home renovations) and creative channels (i.e., channels where individuals create original digital or analogue works of art) more discoverable so that streamers who paint with oils and canvas, mow their lawns, conduct interviews with interesting people, or even play tabletop roleplaying games are easier to find on the platform (Videomaker, 2018).

While there is a wealth of content available on Twitch, it is fair to say that the majority is video game based. The top 100 most popular channels, for example, consist almost entirely of gaming streams (Jia, Shen, Epema, & Iosup, 2016). As other authors have commented (cf. Lin et al., 2019), this seems counterintuitive. If the draw to video games instead of television or film is that they are an interactive medium, then why would people want to remove the interactivity?

The aim of this chapter is to debate that question by illustrating how streaming platforms such as Twitch afford a different flavor of interactivity. Instead of interacting with a game, viewers are interacting real-time with a live streamer and a community of other viewers while still absorbing the content of a game. It has been commented that the appeal of Twitch is the appeal of interacting with a community that shares your interests (Blight, 2016). In this sense, Twitch is not unlike a comic book or sci-fi convention − it is a platform for participatory cultures to engage with each other with a base of shared culture and media. This chapter debates claims that Twitch is a less interactive medium than playing video games by showing how streamers and gaming communities use the platform to socialize and network and, ultimately, interact.

This distinction is the focus of this chapter and will be discussed in the two subsections. First, "The Rise of the Streamer" will focus on how individuals with webcams became celebrities. This will be followed by a discussion of "Twitch and Gaming Communities," which explores the role of Twitch in developing and sustaining gaming communities. A third subsection, "Equal Participation," will provide a brief discussion of disparities in their popularity based on gender and race. The focus of this chapter is to dispel some common misconceptions about the uses and effects of this medium and provide insight into what Twitch is, what it is not, and what it may be in the future.

History of the Streamer

Streamers are now celebrities. A familiar name in many households, Tyler "Ninja" Blevins was named one of *Time Magazine*'s most influential people in 2019 for his Fortnite stream on Twitch (Chalk, 2019). Other personalities, like Dr. DisRespect, have over 3 million followers and earn tens of thousands of dollars a month in sponsorships and subscriptions (Webb, 2019). One such personality that has long since been forgotten is that of lonelygirl15, a YouTube channel formed on June 16, 2006, by a bored 16-year-old named Bree (Lonelygirl15, 2006). Remarkably, the rise of the streamer, influencer, and content creator was made possible through this channel by becoming YouTube's first viral alternate reality game (ARG). The channel quickly gained widespread popularity on YouTube – often to the tune of 500,000 views per video within a week (Cresci, 2016). Lonelygirl15 (LG15) was the first true YouTube celebrity, but the channel, its scandal, and impact on current online professions that revolve around streaming and social media have been largely forgotten. While news media outlets are quick to discuss how important and popular streamers are, they often neglect the important history of how a cultural shift toward streaming happened in the first place.

This section of the chapter aims to remedy this neglect by giving a detailed account of the LG15's impact on modern streaming culture. While the contributions of LG15's channel are many, this section will seek to discuss the two most notable practices it popularized. Not only did it facilitate the first national conversation about the role of authenticity expected from online personalities, but it also established how communities can be built both on online platforms and social media channels. Debates surrounding these practices rose out of LG15's controversy and are still actively discussed today.

The LG15 YouTube channel started out simply – a girl named Bree would talk to a webcam about her daily life in short videos less than 3 minutes long. This format was part of a new genre called the bedroom blog, known as the vlog, in which users would film daily updates on their lives from the privacy of their bedrooms (Aran, Biel, & Gatica-Perez, 2014). LG15's videos included her best friend Daniel, known as Danielbeast (Danielbeast, 2016), who would at times respond to Bree's videos on his own channel, creating a web of content that users followed daily. Bree and Daniel felt so relatable, authentic, and genuine: they talked about teenage crushes, strict parents, and doing their homework. However, before long the lighthearted nature of the videos grew dark as a cult conspiracy was revealed replete with villains, spying, and intrigue. Followers of the channel actively debated over the authenticity and reality of Bree's accounts based on the perceived implausibility of the content. Each uploaded video spurred further speculation on chat rooms and forums online.

Yet while the events felt implausible to some, many viewers maintained belief in the veracity of the videos given the supposed authenticity of Bree and Daniel. Skeptics scoured Bree's MySpace profile and emailed her as well as posted comments on her videos. When viewers received replies back it only served to validate her authenticity. LG15 quickly became the most watched and hotly debated channel on YouTube, with the matter of Bree's authenticity serving as the central question. Three months after the channel's creation, it would be discovered by internet sleuths and reporters (Rushfield, 2006) that Bree was actually Jessica Lee Rose, and her channel was operated by three amateur filmmakers (Heffernan & Zeller, 2006). The videos were fake. The reaction was swift – many viewers felt betrayed. Some became even more invested. Newspaper outlets such as the *New York Times* and *Los Angeles Times* provided daily updates on the scandal. LG15 had thus started the first national conversation surrounding the role of online authenticity.

When the LG15 channel was first published, YouTube and sites such as justin.tv were just getting started, and careers were being created that didn't have names yet: streamer, content creator, and influencer. As such, it was the first time national attention was turned toward the expectations an audience had for those entering into these professions. Even after the videos were exposed as fake, surprisingly the channel became more popular with news of the scandal going viral. It turned out that LG15's sense of amateurism gave a veneer of authenticity that ended up mattering more than the actual reality (Hall, 2015). LG15's continued popularity after the scandal proved that people were willing to accept a false reality as long as the show of authenticity was performed well. The guise of the authentic became a fundamental part of modern social media, YouTube, and streaming itself — broadcasts are performative in substance, but streamers claim them as unscripted, authentic content for their viewers. On the one hand they are not incorrect — viewers are indeed watching streamers perform live. A streamer will say followers' names, film content from their bedrooms, and give real reactions to video games. Yet in truth there is no way of knowing if the displayed names of the streamer are real, if their reactions are sincere, or if the bedroom they stream from is actually in their home — performativity is inherently involved (Pellicone et al., 2017). A streamer can become whatever he or she wishes to be online as long as he or she maintains the façade of authenticity with an online persona.

LG15 also established a working model for the modern streamer to build a strong community of dedicated viewers and patrons that still persists in streaming culture. Part of the appeal streamers have is their direct communication with and accessibility to their audiences. Streamers are expected to answer the chat questions; thank their subscribers; take notice of what content they liked; and, most importantly, build a community surrounding their channel. LG15 successfully established personal connections with viewers by responding individually to comments posted on its videos, emails and direct messages both on YouTube — its primary platform — and on alternative platforms such as its personal website and MySpace. Because YouTube allowed for comments to be left below each uploaded video, it encouraged participation from its viewers. LG15 capitalized on this feature of the website and would not only read the comments but, as Bree, respond to individual users, sometimes dropping a clue relevant to the mystery of the videos, which spurred fans to comment further. It motivated commenters to engage with one another as they exchanged theories, opinions, and support for each other's participation. This type of exposure to an online personality was appealing — having direct access to the content creator themselves turned out to be something audiences wanted.

Today, LG15's techniques of engaging with audiences are industry standards — Instagram influencers regularly engage with their followers, and Twitter celebrities can post direct replies and retweets to fans that are viewed publicly. The streaming community in particular has taken this technique and pushed it to the next level — streamers are expected to be in constant conversation with their community through their live stream both on-camera and through chat as well as participate on Discord and through their social media profiles. In the end, the appeal of streaming goes back to the vlog and the way LG15 utilized it − a streamer is not unlike Bree, sitting in her bedroom, talking with viewers, and responding to posted comments. LG15 met its audience where they were, whether that was through email, social media, or YouTube itself, thus creating a brand of relationship-building that streamers currently use with evidence suggesting that shared experiences online create a deeper sense of community (Sjöblom, & Hamari, 2017).

The impact of LG15's channel is still felt today in how Twitch builds celebrities, creates content, and engages with viewers. The following section builds on the idea of audience engagement by looking at how Twitch fosters the development of communities.

The Good Side of Twitch

As a platform used primarily to share live gameplay, Twitch takes an active role in creating a virtual hub for communities of gamers. This section explores how Twitch is a meeting place for gaming communities by looking first at under which conditions they form and then by discussing the reasons why individual viewers attach themselves to channel followings. The section ends with a brief discussion of exclusionary practices and community guidelines within Twitch.

To begin, context is needed to explain how Twitch brings disparate viewers and gamers together. As discussed in the section above, part of Twitch's role in community building involves the streamer-as-celebrity (Taylor, 2016; Vosmeer et al., 2016). Viewers find streamer "personalities" they enjoy watching, which is not entirely different from how other media consumers attach themselves to reality television or athlete personalities, and then build relationships with other fans of that particular streamer. Of course, this community of streamer fans is not restrained to only Twitch but also employs social media and Discord channels as auxiliary ways of reaching out and communicating.

Aside from wanting to follow Twitch celebrities for the sake of celebrity, viewers also seek out Twitch to witness speed, grace, or general excellence in gameplay. In this sense, watching Twitch is not dissimilar to watching professional sports on television, and thus the development of fan communities is not dissimilar to sports. Take speedrunning as an example of this. Speedrunning, or the practice of competitively completing a game or level in the least amount of time possible, has a large Twitch following as the material itself is exciting to watch (Scully-Blaker, 2016). In addition to finding thrill in the fast-paced action on screen, speedrunning viewers additionally enjoy watching to find hints or tips on how to perfect their own speedrunning attempts. And indeed, learning to be a better player no matter the platform or genre seems to be a popular reason to engage with communities of gamers on Twitch (Vosmeer et al., 2016).

Finally, communities build around Twitch channels based on the sheer social interaction it provides. Watching and interacting with streams and streamers seems to provide parasocial (or one-sided) relationships to ameliorate negative feelings of isolation and loneliness that plague contemporary adult life (Blight, 2016; Lin et al., 2019). Although all channels can be said to espouse the development of parasocial relationships, a strong example of this is the rise of social eating. The stream category of social eating is a reference to a popular South Korean stream style known as "muk-bang" where young people stream themselves eating large quantities of food while chatting to viewers (McWhertor, 2016). The general purpose of these channels, although surely there are viewers who watch for other reasons as well, is to make viewers feel as though they are having a meal with a group of friends. It is by its nature a social act involving eating and chatting – not different to going out to a restaurant or a dinner party with a group of friends, except it happens in an online, virtual space. Muk-bang develops parasocial relationships that help strengthen communities of viewers through the use of chatting and eating.

In addition to enjoying social interactions with streams, stream communities also enjoy being able to have a direct impact on the stream itself and indeed on the streamer's life outside of it. The ways in which viewers can have a direct impact on streams is through spamming chat with phrases or emojis (Karhulahti, 2016); engaging in carnival-like banter or humor (Lin et al., 2019); expressive information sharing about their lives, their interest in a particular game, or their playstyle (Blight, 2016); and money or subscriptions to the streamer (Karhulahti, 2016).

Arguably the most palpable way viewers impact a stream or streamer online and offline is through the exchange of money (Suganuma, 2018). During a live stream (when streamers are broadcasting live), viewers can give a streamer "bits," Twitch's own currency that viewers purchase through an in-stream interface, as a form of tip. Usually Bit donations are small tokens of appreciation, a dollar or two left in a virtual jar to indicate enjoyment, but larger streams feature leaderboards showing the hundreds and sometimes thousands of dollars viewers have tipped. Bits, along with direct donations via PayPal, have an impact on streams by affording streamers the ability to purchase better equipment, create more games, or make streaming their full-time occupation. In effect, this form of patronage allows for communities of viewers to determine which streamers deserve more airtime or more exposure; being able to make streaming a full-time job allows the streamer more time to be on-air and better equipment ensures a higher quality stream that will attract more viewers.

The Bad Side of Twitch

Although this chapter has predominantly focused on the positive aspects of community-building through Twitch, our debate would be incomplete if we left out the ways in which the platform, intentionally or not, creates and maintains boundaries of exclusion that make it difficult for certain groups of people to participate.

Women, in particular, can find Twitch communities to be unwelcoming. In her work on women in e-sports, Emma Witkowski (2018) has found that high performance athletes are stigmatized as "girl gamers" and are thought to have lower skill or ability by communities of viewers regardless of their actual ability on stream. The term "girl gamer" is often used as a way to gatekeep women out of engaging with games in general or streaming more particularly. The assumption behind the term, particularly on Twitch, is that communities only coalesce around women streamers because of their looks or sexual availability – the underlying concept being that a woman playing games has only her body or sexuality to offer viewers and no real skill in gameplay.

While we may expect communities of male viewers to use this term, it is unfortunately common to see other women use girl gamer to exclude women, too. Ruvalcaba and colleagues (2018) found that in highly competitive situations where sexism is already present and there are low numbers of women participating, for example in e-sports or in trying to achieve financial sustainability on Twitch, women will see other women as a threat to their success. Using terms like girl gamer is a way to undermine the legitimacy of other women streamers and drive viewers to "authentic" (i.e., male) gamer streams.

In addition to the community-policing detailed above, the safeguards and rules developed by Twitch, also known as community guidelines, help police and enforce the Twitch community. The community guidelines specifically ban breaking the law; account suspension evasion; self-destructive behavior; violence and threats; hateful conduct and harassment; unauthorized sharing of private information; impersonation; spam, scams, and other malicious content; nudity, pornography, and other sexual content; extreme violence; gore; other obscene conduct; and intellectual property (Twitch.tv 2019). Although these guidelines are consistent with most social norms, they represent Twitch taking action to police, control, and define the community that engages with its platform (Suganuma, 2018). To be a part of a Twitch community is, according to its guidelines, to be respectful and inclusive. Of course, as the example above and the following section below illustrate, members do not always follow these guidelines.

Much has been said in social and academic discourse about the role of sexism and racism in streaming culture and what responsibility platforms such as Twitch, YouTube, and Mixer have in generating equal spaces for vulnerable minority groups (Fox & Tang, 2017). Yet absent from the discourse is how streaming platforms exacerbate income inequality and economic status through their monetization methods and structure. Financial instability creates and reinforces barriers that prevent streamers from full and equal participation in streaming communities. The methods streamers use to profit can also aggravate stereotypes toward minority groups. While this conversation focuses on Twitch and pulls data specific to the United States, there may be applicability to other platforms and countries.

Streaming has appeal for similar reasons to other forms of gig economy work – the barrier to entry seems low – all you need is a console, a webcam, and a personality. While several years ago streamers were able to establish their channels without the need for professional production quality, the realities have changed with Twitch's rise in popularity – the more well-produced the stream, the more motivation there is for a viewer to keep watching. In actuality, consoles range from $200–$400 and new titles can cost $60 each. If streamers play free games, they may require subscription services, which adds cost over time. Most professional streamers transition to the use of PCs because of the freedom it provides in building stream quality, yet many require two computers to operate – one for the game, another for streaming. These computers can cost thousands of dollars for reliable hardware and don't include the peripherals, lighting, sound, or video-editing software. The cost of creating a Twitch stream has no limit for those with money to spend – Harris Heller, a YouTuber who reviews stream equipment and provides Twitch advice, admitted that over the last decade he spent over $30,000 for equipment (Alpha Gaming, 2019).

In addition, having reliable internet is mandatory in order to successfully stream. Researchers have noted that access to the internet is tied to income status, especially as it relates to race (Rutten et al., 2012; Talukdar & Gauri, 2011). Furthermore, while Blacks and Latinos were equally likely to have access to the internet, both groups were less likely to have access than were Whites (Campos-Castillo, 2015). Data from the Federal Communications Commission (FCC) report that 24 million Americans still lack access to fixed terrestrial broadband speeds of 25 Mbps/3 Mbps, the minimum qualification for usable internet access. Fourteen million in rural communities and 1.2 Americans living in tribal areas lack broadband at speed of 10 Mbps/3 Mbps. They also acknowledged that those with less access to broadband services are more likely to live in poverty and have less than the median income household in the United States (FCC, 2018). Due to Twitch relying on the internet both for streamers and viewers, lower-income populations and minority groups are less likely to have access that allows them to reliably stream.

While internet and start-up costs come at the expense of the streamer, they have yet to make a profit upon starting a channel, especially due to a lack of affiliated or partnered status – designations Twitch grants to guarantee a revenue split on subscriptions. Streamers must first prove they have an audience, then apply by invitation for affiliate or partner status – yet there's no guarantee that Twitch will accept the applications. Of equal importance is consideration of the time spent in producing streams – to consistently set up and monitor a stream, engage in live broadcasts, and then curate those streams for "post-able" content requires several hours a week. Many streamers also spend time creating overlays, panels, and animations for their channels in order to properly market their broadcasts and personal brand.

Such costs establish a barrier to entry for many who are given the promise of affordability but are confronted with the reality cost. With only 39% of Americans having at least $1,000 available in their emergency savings (Garcia, 2019), it is clear that for many the possibility of eclipsing start-up costs is low. Out of the reported 2 million streamers broadcasting on Twitch each month, 150,000 of these are affiliated and only 27,000 are partnered (Perez, 2018; Twitch Interactive, 2020). Broken down, those percentages show that only 0.075% of streamers are able to gain affiliate status and 0.0135% gain partnerships. Such percentages reveal that few get to benefit from a revenue split with Twitch. Furthermore, after gaining affiliate status, a streamer is required to generate $100 in profit before he or she sees a paycheck.

With all of these factors considered, the odds of finding monetary success on Twitch for the economically unstable are slim to none. Equal participation on Twitch depends on having the financial means to support oneself while building a community and personal brand, which many lack. Furthermore, monetization methods used by streamers prevent full and equal participation while simultaneously granting it. For example, there are three ways to generate income on the Twitch platform itself: subscriptions, donations, and bits. Monthly subscriptions to a streamer give special privileges to those who pay depending on the tier they choose, with the cost differentials coming in at $4.99, $9.99, and $24.99 respectively. As stated above, half the profit is split with Twitch. The motivations to subscribe to a streamer are varied, including but not limited to private access to subscriber-only streams and admittance to the streamer's Discord channel.

However, one of the most popular motivations to subscribe includes the use of a streamer's emotes. Similar to emojis on smartphones, emotes are used in chat and message features on Twitch. These emotes are personally made by or for the streamer with the subscription tier determining the number of emotes a viewer receives. Emotes are integrated into the lexicon, vocabulary, and culture on Twitch in a way that promotes and establishes communities around streamer personalities. Yet, as was reported in 2019, these emotes have been used to promote racist attitudes and stereotypes on Twitch, with users using them in chat on different streamers channels to harass others. For instance, prominent streamers such as Hasan Pike and Asmongold have reported viewers spamming emotes of black people and Kentucky Fried Chicken buckets to insinuate racist jokes and attitudes (Grayson, 2019). Furthermore, Twitch's Global Emotes, emotes available to all Twitch users, have far fewer women and minority representations. Twitch community guidelines states that hateful conduct based on designations such as race, ethnicity, and gender are prohibited and that action will be taken against such behavior (Twitch.tv, 2019). However, constant monitoring and swift responses from Twitch have been inconsistent. Emotes serve as a strong motivator for subscribers to donate money to a streamer and promote his or her brand but can also lead to the abuse and harassment of minority groups.

Another form of monetization, bits, may not overtly suggest sexist stereotypes but they do draw associations that unconsciously make it more difficult for the female streaming community to participate. Bits seems to replicate the use of similar features on pornography sites to cheer for camgirls – women who film pornographic activity online for a live audience (Convery, 2017). Earlier sections detailed the negative association attached to girl gamers and how this terminology has damaged equal participation for female streamers – such associations are linked to camgirls and their work. Yet female streamers have not inherently signaled consent to sexualize their content like camgirls because they choose to broadcast online. While Twitch's Community Guidelines clearly prohibit such bias aimed toward women, the continued existence of bits highlights how these associations can be reinforced to earn profit.

The final way in which streamers earn an income on Twitch is through the use of donations. Streamers provide a link on their channel to an external transaction site, such as Paypal, which viewers then visit to donate money. All proceeds go directly to the streamer and the viewer gets recognition by a verbal shout out or an animation that appears on screen. Yet donations are made at the discretion of the viewer, and data released by Paypal in 2018 concluded that women receive half of what male streamers make. Additionally, they reported that the gender pay gap from streaming donations was the largest in the United States out of all countries surveyed (Bello, 2018). Twitch does not monitor donations since these transactions are processed on external sites, but such disparities drawn on gendered lines insinuate that systemic discrimination exists on the platform.

There are many other areas of economic disparity on Twitch that have yet to be considered. Barriers as they relate to viewers and their ability to participate, as well as how sponsorships and brand endorsements figure into the streaming landscape, should enter the conversation. Not included within this discussion are the harassment and economic impact on lesbian, gay, bisexual, transgender, and queer/questioning minority groups, which deserves thorough research and thoughtful discussion. However, it is clear that becoming a streamer on Twitch is influenced by economic mobility, making it more difficult for those in lower income brackets to participate. Furthermore, monetization methods such as subscriptions, bits, and donations can be used against minority groups and garner stereotypes that damage the ability to create equal opportunity for all streamers, whatever their background or identification.

Examining these economic disparities on platforms serves to show that streaming is a microscope for other active debates surrounding tech: what responsibility do platforms have in maintaining a healthy relationship between free speech versus harassment? Is the marketing of a seemingly convenient career path as a streamer false advertising or just ethically dubious? Are the terms and conditions that users and streamers sign sufficient enough to clear platforms of certain responsibilities in response the inequality outlined above? Furthermore, are platforms bolstering structures of inequality by marketing diversity? As streaming grows and experiences its renaissance, these questions cannot help but rise to the surface. Unfortunately, unless these open debates are addressed, new streamers will continue coming to their platforms expecting an equal opportunity to gain success in the wild west of online gaming – little do they know that with such tensions these opportunities may have already dissolved.

Conclusion

As an ever changing website with new personalities, games, and trends emerging constantly, it is difficult to write a definitive chapter on Twitch and participatory culture. What this chapter provides is a singular account of how streamers and streaming media came to be, the appeal of this media to fan communities, and how limited access to resources and streaming technology can create exclusionary practices. From this discussion, it can be concluded that Twitch is currently a strong aspect of gaming culture and participatory culture at large. And while the effects of this strength are likely to grow and change over time, its impact will always be felt.

References

Alpha Gaming. (2019). Home [AlphaGaming]. Retrieved from https://www.youtube.com/channel/UCATWC1JSlhzmYeDbjnS8WwA.

Aran, O., Biel, J., & Gatica-Perez, D. (2014). Broadcasting oneself: Visual discovery of vlogging styles. *IEEE Transactions on Multimedia, 16*(1), 201–215.

Bello, A. (2018, May 29). PayPal 2018 gaming insights: The gender divide, esports and more. Retrieved from https://www.paypal.com/stories/us/paypal-2018-gaming-insights-the-gender-divide-esports-and-more.

Berry, S. (2018, August 8). Non-gaming Twitch channels may see spike in viewers after update. Videomaker. Retrieved from https://www.videomaker.com/non-gaming-twitch-channels-may-see-spike-in-traffic-after-update.

Blight, M. G. (2016). *Relationships to video game streamers: Examining gratifications, parasocial relationships, fandom, and community affiliation online*. (PhD Dissertation). University of Milwaukee.

Campos-Castillo, C. (2015). Revisiting the first-level digital divide in the United States: Gender and race/ethnicity patterns, 2007–2012. *Social Science Computer Review, 33*(4), 423–439.

Chalk, A. (2019). Ninja makes *Time*'s "Most Influential People" list for 2019. PC Gamer. Retrieved from https://www.pcgamer.com/ninja-makes-times-most-influential-people-list-for-2019/ Accessed on:1/1/2020.

Convery, S. (2017, January 3). The women who make a living gaming on Twitch. Retrieved from https://www.theguardian.com/technology/2017/jan/03/women-make-living-gaming-twitch.

Cresci, E. (2016, June 16). Lonelygirl15: How one mysterious vlogger changed the internet. The Guardian. Retrieved from https://www.theguardian.com/technology/2016/jun/16/lonelygirl15-bree-video-blog-youtube.

Danielbeast (2016). Home [Danielbeast]. Retrieved from https://www.youtube.com/user/Danielbeast.

Federal Communications Commission. (2018, February 05). 2018 broadband deployment report. Retrieved August 13, 2019, Retrieved from https://www.fcc.gov/reports-research/reports/broadband-progress-reports/2018-broadband-deployment-report.

Finney Rutten, L. J., Davis, T., Beckjord, E. B., Blake, K., Moser, R. P., & Hesse, B. W. (2012). Picking up the pace: Changes in method and frame for the Health Information National Trends Survey (2011–2014). *Journal of Health Communication, 17*(8), 979–989.

Fox, J., & Tang, W. Y. (2017). Women's experiences with general and sexual harassment in online video games: Rumination, organizational responsiveness, withdrawal, and coping strategies. *New Media & Society, 19*(8), 1290–1307. Retrieved from https://doi.org/10.1177/1461444816635778.

Garcia, A. (2019, January 16). Survey: Most Americans wouldn't cover a $1K emergency with savings. Bankrate. Retrieved from https://www.bankrate.com/banking/savings/financial-security-january-2019/.

Grayson, N. (2019, June 5). Twitch still hasn't fixed its racist emote problem. Retrieved from https://kotaku.com/twitch-still-hasnt-fixed-its-racist-emote-problem-1835253131.

Hall, K. (2015). The authenticity of social-media performance: Lonelygirl15 and the amateur brand of young-girlhood. *Women & Performance: A Journal of Feminist Theory, 25*, 1–15.

Heffernan, V., & Zeller, Tom. (2006, September 13). The lonelygirl that really wasn't. *New York Times*. Retrieved from https://www.nytimes.com/.

Jia, A. L., Shen, S., Epema, D. H., & Iosup, A. (2016). When game becomes life: The creators and spectators of online game replays and live streaming. *ACM Transactions on Multimedia Computing, Communications, and Applications (TOMM), 12*(4), 47.

Karhulahti, V. M. (2016). Prank, troll, gross and gore: Performance issues in esport live-streaming. In *DiGRA/FDG, 1*, 1–13.

Lin, J. H. T., Bowman, N., Lin, S. F., & Chen, Y. S. (2019). Setting the digital stage: Defining game streaming as an entertainment experience. *Entertainment Computing, 31*, 100309.

Lonelygirl15(2006). Home [lonelygirl15]. Retrieved from https://www.youtube.com/user/lonelygirl15.

Lonelygirl15 exposes the Net's illogical sense of community. (2006). *Eureka Street, 16* (13), 21–21. doi: https://doi.org/BRYCE DALLAS HOWARD.

McWhertor, M. 2016. Twitch now lets you watch people eat: Enter the muk-bang. *Kotaku*. Retrieved from https://www.polygon.com/2016/6/29/12063430/twitch-social-eating-food-streams-mukbang Accessed on: 14 August 2019.

Pellicone, A., Ahn, J., Clegg, T., Kirschenbaum, M., Kraus, K., & Vitak, J. (2017). *Performing play: Cultural production on Twitch.tv*, ProQuest Dissertations and Theses.

Perez, S. (2018, February 6). Twitch now has 27K Partners and 150K affiliates making money from their videos. Retrieved from https://techcrunch.com/2018/02/06/twitch-now-has-27k-partners-and-150k-affiliates-making-money-from-their-videos/.

Rushfield, R. (2006, September 9). Lonelygirl15's revelation: It's all just part of the show. *Los Angeles Times*. Retrieved from https://www.latimes.com/.

Ruvalcaba, O., Shulze, J., Kim, A., Berzenski, S. R., & Otten, M. P. (2018). Women's experiences in esports: Gendered differences in peer and spectator feedback during competitive video game play. *Journal of Sport and Social Issues, 42*(4), 295–311.

Scully-Blaker, R. (2016). On becoming "Like eSports": Twitch as a platform for the speedrunning community. Paper presented at the 1st joint conference of DiGRA and FDG. p. 1-2. Retrieved from https://e-channel.med.utah.edu/wp-content/uploads/2017/02/paper_193.pdf.

Sjoblom, M., Hamari, J. (2017). Why do people watch others play video games? An empirical study on the motivations of Twitch users. *Computers in Human Behavior, 75*, 985–996.

Suganuma, N. K. (2018). *An ethnography of the Twitch.tv streamer and viewer relationship*. California State University, Long Beach.

Talukdar, D., & Gauri, D. K. (2011). Home internet access and usage in the USA: Trends in the socio-economic digital divide. *Communications of the Association for Information Systems, 28*(1), 7.

Taylor, N. (2016). Play to the camera: Video ethnography, spectatorship, and e-sports. *Convergence, 22*(2), 115–130.

Taylor, T. L. (2012). *Raising the stakes: E-sports and the professionalization of computer gaming*. MIT Press.

Tepper, T. (2018, December 12). Most Americans don't have enough savings to cover a $1K emergency. Retrieved from https://www.bankrate.com/banking/savings/financial-security-0118/.

Twitch.tv (2019). Community guidelines. Accessed from: https://www.twitch.tv/p/legal/community-guidelines/ Accessed on8/14/2019.

Twitch Interactive, Inc. (2020). Frequently asked questions. Retrieved August 13, 2019, from https://www.twitch.tv/p/partners/faq/.

Vosmeer, M., Ferri, G., Schouten, B., & Rank, S. (2016). Changing roles in gaming: Twitch and new gaming audiences. In Proceedings of 1st International Joint Conference of DiGRA and FDG, Dundee, Scotland, UK, 1–2.

Webb, K. (2019). From Ninja to Dr. Disrespect, these are the 10 most popular channels on Twitch. *Business Insider*. Retrieved 16 August 2019, from: https://www.businessinsider.com/top-twitch-streamers-by-follower-count-ninja-shroud-tfue-2019-6.

Witkowski, E. (2012). On the digital playing field: How we "do sport" with networked computer games. *Games and Culture, 7*(5), 349–374.

Witkowski, E. (2018). Doing/undoing gender with the girl gamer in high-performance play. In *Feminism in play* (pp. 185–203). Palgrave Macmillan, Cham.

6

PLAYING TO WIN

The Global Esports Industry and Key Issues

Stephanie Orme

Competitive video game play – also known as esports – has come a long way from its humble origins in arcades and personal computer (PC) cafes, having evolved into a multibillion dollar global industry today. Despite its allure for aspiring professional players – and opportunistic investors – the world of esports remains misunderstood by many. In this chapter, Orme offers an overview of the global esports industry while engaging with some key debates surrounding esports, from what "counts" as esports to mounting concerns about cheating and corruption. The chapter begins with a discussion of what constitutes esports, followed by a brief description of the various league and team systems that permeate much of esports and how professional players fit into that landscape. From there, Orme discusses some of the major social issues related to esports, such as a professionalization of video game play and esports' symbiotic relationship with video game live-streaming. Finally, Orme homes in on the physical and mental impacts that esports are already found to be having on its players, from anxiety and burnout to athletic injuries.

The South Philadelphia Sports Complex is home to Philadelphia's professional sports teams for the national hockey, baseball, football and basketball leagues and associations as well as the National Collegiate Athletic Association. In 2021, those teams will have a new neighbor: the Philadelphia Fusion, the city's professional team for the first-person shooter video game Overwatch (Blizzard Entertainment, 2016). The Fusion announced plans to construct a $50 million arena designed specifically for esports, with its own training facility and broadcast studio – the first purpose-built stadium for esports in the Western hemisphere (Khalid, 2019). The Overwatch League (OWL) is an international competitive league consisting of 20 city-based teams. Teams play a 280-match regular season that culminates with playoffs each fall. OWL franchises have sold for over $20 million to the likes of the

Houston Rockets and Robert Kraft, with franchises being valued between $60–$80 million dollars, depending on the city (Ozanian, Settemi, & Perez 2018).

Today's esports scene, with its arena sellouts and corporate sponsorships, is a stark contrast from the local area network tournaments hosted at the local Blockbuster in the 1990s. Naturally, esports' rise to prominence has captured the attention of many, from game studies scholars to investors. This chapter provides an overview of esports, from its humble origins of one-on-one competitions to the multimillion-dollar spectacle that it has become today. I begin by defining esports – namely, what differentiates it from traditional sport as well as regular gaming. Next, I describe the global landscape of esports, including how esports is organized into various teams, leagues, and tournaments. Finally, I will discuss some of the existing scholarship on the social and health-based effects that esports has on its participants, audiences, and society at large.

What Is Esports?

Because esports shares many of the conventions of physical sports, esports is often defined in relation to them. However, esports is also distinct from traditional sport, in that *play*, in this instance, occurs through computing. The complexity of these interlocking systems, as well as the novelty of the industry, make defining esports contentious (Jin, 2010). At its simplest, esports can be understood as *organized video game competitions*. Competitive gaming differs from normal video game play in that players must outperform their competition in solving an in-game challenge using game-specific strategies while deftly manipulating a mouse and/or keyboard to execute tactics. Heaven (2014) captures this sense of required skill in his description of competitive *StarCraft* (Blizzard Entertainment, 1998), a sci-fi game that combines real-time strategy with resource management:

> To do as well as the pros, you must also achieve an extremely rapid rate of keyboard and mouse inputs. Some players carry out more than 300 such actions a minute, rising to 10 a second when up against it. Add in the need to think strategically and outwit your opponent by pre-empting their moves, and the top players start to look superhuman. (Heaven, 2014, para. 10–11, as cited in Jenny, Manning, Keiper, & Olrich, 2016)

The most popular esports games – from both a player and spectator standpoint – emphasize skills such as quick reflexes, hand-eye coordination, precision, strategy, and teamwork. Popular esports game genres include first-person shooters (e.g., *Overwatch* [Counter-Strike: Global Offensive. [Computer software] 2012]), multiplayer-online battle arenas (e.g., *League of Legends* [Riot Games, 2012], *Dota 2*, Defense of the Ancients [streamer/dogdog. Dota 2. [Computer software] 2013]), online card games (e.g., Hearthstone [Blizzard Entertainment, 2014]), and sports-themed games (e.g., *FIFA* [EA Sports], *NBA 2K* [2K Sports]).

Sports Games and Esports

A common misconception is that esports refers to sports-simulation video games played in a "sedentary" context (Kim & Ross, 2006), such as the *FIFA* soccer series or *Madden NFL* (EA Sports, 1988) football series. In these games, players control a character – in some cases, modeled after actual athletes – in simulated matches. Although these games deal with sports in terms of content, the game itself is not "esports." That said, many sedentary sports video games, like *NBA 2K*, for instance, have formed their own esports leagues, in which players competitively play the game.

The Scope of Esports

Although it remains something of an enigma to many cultural outsiders, esports is a multimillion dollar global industry. Newzoo (2019) calculates that global esports revenues are poised to top $1 billion in 2019, with North American generating the biggest share of revenue at $489 million. The Chinese and South Korean markets are expected to bring in 19% and 6% of the total revenue, respectively, with the remaining 38% scattered across other markets, including Europe. The majority of revenue comes in the form of advertising and corporate sponsorship but also includes broadcast agreements, ticket sales, merchandise, and fees collected by game publishers (Newzoo, 2019).

The audience for esports continues to grow at staggering rates as well. South Korea has been televising esports for almost 20 years, with its own stations dedicated to reporting on esports news and events (Jin, 2010). Elsewhere, the majority of viewership continues to come from online platforms such as Twitch and YouTube or regional platforms like China's Huya, dubbed "the Twitch of China" (Braithwaite, 2018). Founded in 2011 with the purpose of broadcasting video game play, Twitch – acquired by Amazon in 2014 – is arguably the home of esports broadcasting today. Twitch regularly broadcasts major esports tournaments, including *Dota 2's* The International and *League of Legends'* League Champion Series (LCS) World Cup. The 2018 LCS World Cup drew 99.6 million viewers for the finals, according to Riot Games. For comparison, the 2018 Super Bowl garnered 103 million viewers – a difference of just 3.4 million (Mickunas, 2019). In the United States, traditional media companies are starting to invest more heavily into esports broadcasting. In 2018, Disney secured an exclusive multiyear contract with *Overwatch* publisher Activision Blizzard to air *Overwatch League* matches on ABC, ESPN, and Disney XD. The Grand Finals marked the first time live competitive gaming had been aired on primetime on ESPN (Fogel, 2018).

The global success of esports can also be measured by the increasing size of prize pools from major esports tournaments. In July 2019, 16-year-old

Pennsylvanian Kyle Giersdorf secured the first solo-win at the inaugural Fortnite World Cup, nabbing an astonishing $3 million prize. The amount exceeds the take-home for the winners of several traditional sport competitions, including the 2019 PGA, Masters, and Wimbledon tournaments (ESPN, 2019). *Fortnite's* publisher, Epic Games, awarded a total of $30 million in prizes throughout the tournament (Shieber, 2019), which garnered over 2 million concurrent viewers across Twitch and YouTube (live streaming platforms; Watercutter, 2019). That same week, the *Dota 2* tournament, The International, shattered the record for the largest prize pool for any single esports event, surpassing the $30 million mark, largely through crowd-funding (Stubbs, 2019).

Leagues of Their Own: How the Esports Industry Is Organized

Esports shares many of the structural concepts of traditional sports, such as leagues and tournaments; however, the esports industry is even more complex, with many esports companies assuming multiple roles. In this section, I will discuss some of the key structural components of the industry.

Tournaments

Tournaments have been part of the esports ecosystem since before "esports" was part of the lexicon – the earliest forms being "high score" competitions as opposed to one-on-one or team-based competitions (Taylor, 2012). With increased internet connectivity in the 1990s, online gaming tournaments caught on, with *Counter-Strike* and *Quake* (GT Interactive) being among the most popular tournament games. The 1990s also saw the formation of several large tournaments, including the Nintendo World Championships and the international fighting games tournament, Evolution Championship Series (EVO). The 2000s would usher in a new era for esports globally. PC bangs – or internet cafes – popularized PC gaming in South Korea, an interest the government nourished by creating the Korean E-sports Association to organize and televise esports events. It was the *StarCraft* pro-league's finals match, which drew an audience of 10,000 spectators to the beaches of Busan, that made it clear esports tournaments had surpassed the days of local internet cafes (Mozur, 2014).

Today, tournaments range from amateur weekend events at local venues to international, and even multi-week, affairs that sell out arenas. The structure of tournaments varies from game to game, and league to league, but the general principle involves pitting players (either solo or as part of a team) against one another in elimination matches, culminating in a championship match with prize money.

Leagues and Esports Organizations

Today's esports industry consists of dozens of professional leagues organized around specific video games. At present, these leagues are managed by a handful of large companies who host branded amateur and pro-level tournaments. The oldest and largest of these organizations, ESL (formerly known as Electronic Sports League), currently manages nine professional leagues for *Counter Strike: Global Offensive (CS:GO), Gears of War* (Microsoft Gears of War. [Computer software] 2006), *Guild Wars 2* (NCSoft, 2012), *Halo 5: Guardians* (Microsoft Halo 5: Guardians. [Computer software] 2015), *Hearthstone, Mortal Kombat* (Midway Games, 1992), *Overwatch, Rocket* League (Psyonix, 2015), and *Tom Clancy's Rainbow Six Siege* (Unisoft, 2015). Other established esports organizations include Major League Gaming (MLG), which predominately hosts North American tournaments, and the Korea e-Sports Association (KeSPA) in South Korea.

Organizations like ESL and MLG will often partner with game publishers to host competitions for their respective games. For example, ESL teamed up with Epic Games to host a $600 Fortnite tournament at the Intel Extreme Masters Katowice Major 2019, a *CS:GO* championship tournament (Chalk, 2019). Whereas these tournaments typically last a few days, more and more game developers and publishers have begun creating their own leagues that run full-length seasons, playoffs, and finals. In 2018, Blizzard Entertainment started the OWL, the premier league for international *Overwatch* competition. As of 2019, the OWL is composed of 20 teams representing cities in the United States, Canada, China, Europe, and South Korea. The competitive season spans the full year, with teams playing 28 matches during the regular season. Traditional sport organizations have also caught onto the popularity of esports: 2018 saw the launch of the NBA 2K League, which is jointly backed by the game's publisher, 2K, and the NBA. Similarly, EA Sports, the publisher behind the *FIFA* soccer games, has partnered with Major League Soccer to form Electronic Major League Soccer (eMLS) (Sarkar, 2018).

Teams and Players

As with traditional sports, esports organizations have their own team owners, coaches, and player contracts. Teams dedicate themselves to a specific game, and large esports organizations might oversee teams for several different games. Team Liquid, for instance, is a multiregional esports organization that boasts professional teams in 14 games, from competitive *Super Smash Bros.* (Nintendo) to *PlayerUnknown's Battlegrounds* (PUBG Corporation). The size of a roster for a particular team depends on the nature of the game.

Contracts stipulate many of the same items as professional athletes, from working conditions to sponsorships and salary. *League of Legends* publisher Riot Games was the first esports organization to offer players in its LCS league regular salaries, in an effort to make professional esports careers more viable (Heitner, 2018). Today, the base minimum salary for LCS players is reportedly $70,000, with the average being "somewhere north of $300,000," nearly double the average amount from just two years prior (Patterson, 2019) – comparable to salaries of Major League Soccer players (Heitner, 2018).

In addition to regular salaries, esports players earn revenue through tournament placings, sponsorships, and streaming. The prize pool for tournaments largely depends on the size of the tournament and the game itself. Historically, *Dota 2* boasts the largest amounts of tournament earnings, by far, having doled out almost $182 million to date, followed by *CS:GO* at $80.4 million ("Top games," 2020). German *Dota 2* pro Kuro "KuroKy" Takhasomi is currently the highest earner of tournament winnings, having pocketed over $4 million over his 10-year career. His biggest single payout was over $2.1 million for winning The International in 2017. Smaller, but still formidable, tournaments award amounts ranging from $500 to $500,000 (http://esportsearnings.com).

As the prize pools for major tournaments continue to escalate, so, too, does the value of esports to investors. Major companies including Intel, Coca-Cola, Red Bull, Mountain Dew, T-Mobile, and even Audi have invested in advertising and sponsoring esports events. Further still, many directly sponsor teams, providing them with branded equipment, uniforms, housing, and other amenities. American internet and cable provider Xfinity Comcast not only sponsors the ESL organization but also the team Evil Geniuses, which is one of the top ranked teams in *League of Legends* and *Dota 2*, among others. Wireless carrier T-Mobile recently became a sponsor for esports organizations TSM and Cloud 9 (Meola, 2018a). In 2019, Nike make headlines when it announced its four-year contract with the League of Legends Pro League (LPL) in China. Nike will supply all 16 teams in the tournament with sneakers and apparel, including jerseys (Summers, 2019). As with traditional sports, merchandise in the form of jerseys and other apparel becomes another source of revenue for teams and organizations.

Finally, many players supplement their income by live-streaming on platforms like Twitch or YouTube in their off time. Streamers earn revenue through monthly subscribers and donations and can monetize their channels through advertising and product sponsorships as well. David "Dog" Caero, a professional *Hearthstone* player for Team Liquid, is estimated to have over 2,800 subscribers on Twitch, which means he earns between $7,000–$9,800 a month in revenue, on top of income from tournaments, sponsorships, and his salary ("DogDog," 2019).

Social Impacts of Esports

As general interest in esports has risen, so, too, has the amount of scholarship being produced on the industry and surrounding culture of esports. The nascent literature, spanning topics from embodiment (Ekdahl & Ravn, 2018) to consumer

Andrews & Ritzer, 2018) reflects the complex ecosystem of esports. This section highlights research on the sociocultural and psychological impacts of esports on players, spectators, and society at large.

Reconstituting Play

One of the major implications of esports on social behavior is the transformation of gaming – a leisure activity – into a professional endeavor. Taylor (2012) has discussed in great detail the many layers "professionalizing" competitive gaming – from the creation and enforcement of rules governing play to the ways that broadcasting influences what makes a "watchable" game. Drawing on Caillois' (2001) argument that professionalizing traditional sport corrupts leisurely play, Seo and Jung (2016) explain that the extrinsic benefits (e.g., money, sponsorships) involved in competitive gaming challenge the historically perceived divide between "pure" play and labor.

Social Engagement Through Spectatorship

Seo and Jung (2016) urge us to shift conceptions of computer game play away from a solitary player interacting with an interface to understand it in the context of broader social activities. They see esports as "an assemblage of consumption practices, where consumers actualize and sustain the eSports phenomenon through their engagement with the interconnected nexuses of playing, watching and governing of eSports [sic]" (Seo & Jung, 2016, p. 637). As Taylor (2012) has noted, playing esports games allows esports consumers to develop specialized knowledge that aids them in watching esports events and even organizing their own. Innovative platforms for viewing esports events offer audiences new ways of engaging with esports, beyond passive spectatorship. Platforms like Twitch feature live chat feeds, which encourage participation with the larger community of spectators (Su & Shih, 2011). This also transforms spectators into commentators, further blurring the lines between roles in esports consumption and production. In 2019, the Overwatch League introduced a feature that allows spectators to choose the camera angle for matches (Moore, 2019), giving audiences more tools for shaping their own consumption practices (Seo & Jung, 2016).

Cheating and Corruption

Competition inevitably provokes concerns about cheating and corruption, and esports is no exception. While cheating has long been part of gaming culture (Consalvo, 2009), incentivizing superior performance through monetary awards, sponsorships, and contracts with elite organizations imbues esports with a level of pressure absent from leisurely play. For some, that pressure proves too much. Thiborg and Carlsson (2010) describe how the centrality of "fairness" to sport is challenged by technological cheats in games. Using *Counter-Strike* as an example, they point to cheats such as "Wallhacks," which permit players to see through walls, giving them a competitive edge. Enforcing rules becomes challenging in cyberspaces due to pluralistic understanding of laws and regulations (Thiborg & Carlsson, 2010). For example, Carter and Gibbs (2013) found competitive *EVE Online* (Simon & Schuster Interactive, 2003) actually welcomes technological exploits, to the point where players accept it as part of "*eveSports*" culture.

Yet cheating in esports is not limited to technological workarounds. The emergence of esports gambling (a logical progression on the competitive sport trajectory esports has followed so far) has already been tied to corrupt behavior in esports. Grove and Krejcik (2015) identify three main categories of esports gambling: sportsbook wagering, fantasy esports, and in-game item wagering. Whereas sportsbooks and fantasy leagues are closely aligned with traditional sport, in-game item wagering is a new breed of gambling and a lucrative one – with an estimated value of $2.5 million in 2015 (Grove & Krejcik, 2015). In-game item wagering treats items as currency, which can be traded with other players or, in the cases of games like *CS:GO* and *Dota 2*, exported to external marketplaces. The most popular form of betting in the *CS:GO* community is known as "skin-betting." Weapons skins, which change the appearance of various weapons in *CS:GO*, can be earned by playing the game, traded with players, or purchased with real currency. Skins have different values, upwards of hundreds of dollars. Players can sync their Steam accounts to a third-party betting site that lets them wager their skins on online casino games like roulette or slots. Skins won in bets can be used to make further bets or sold for real-world money (Meola, 2018b).

Esports gambling with in-game items poses challenges for regulation as the entire betting process occurs through a digital market and uses intangible currency (Hardenstein, 2017). However, this lack of transparency and player identification has already resulted in several skin-betting scandals. Perhaps the highest profile incident was between 2014 and 2015 when two prominent *CS:GO* teams, iBUYPOWER (IBP) and NetCodeGuides.com, were accused of match-fixing. IBP, the heavy favorite, drew suspicion for mediocre game play and nonsensical strategies – suspicion that was further fueled by the "substantial number of high value items won from that match" by the founder of NetCodeGuides.com and several IBP players (Godfrey, 2018). Matchfixing continues to plague the esports industry despite efforts to regulate and lifetime bans for offending players (Wilding, 2019). Macey and Hamari (2018) found that viewing esports is strongly associated with a tendency to gamble on esports. As esports continues to be mainstreamed, we will likely see a corresponding rise in esports gambling, necessitating more transparency and regulation in esports gambling practices.

of Esports on Health and Well-Being

The literature on health benefits and concerns related to esports is scant. With career esports competitors still being a relatively recent phenomenon, it is impossible to make assessments of long-term health effects. There is an abundance of scholarship, however, on the general subject of health outcomes from leisurely video game play (Jones, Scholes, Johnson, Katsikitis, & Carras 2014). We can infer that many of the same effects from playing video games, in general, apply to certain esports contexts as well.

Physical Benefits and Concerns of Esports

Competitive video game play undeniably rewards players with the quickest reflexes, highest manual dexterity, and superior hand-eye coordination (Rambusch, Jakobsson, & Pargman, 2007). In their study of over 850,000 online computer game players, Stafford and Dewar (2014) found that practicing a game resulted in increased performance, suggesting that players do acquire cerebral skill and improve performance through playing video games. Granic, Lobel, and Engels (2014) found that certain types of games can enhance cognitive functions, including problem-solving skills, spatial reasoning skills, and creativity. A meta-analysis of studies on game play and cognition among older adults (Toril, Reales, & Ballesteros, 2014) showed that older adults can improve their reaction time, attention, memory, and global cognition through video game play.

Motion-based video games (MBVGs) – which use motion-sensing technology and software to detect and simulate physical activity made by the player, reproducing their movements onscreen through an avatar (Jenny, Hushman, & Hushman, 2013) – stimulate physical activity such as balance, cardiovascular health, strength, and balance (Oh & Yang, 2010). Examples include the *Dance Dance Revolution* (Konami) dancing and rhythm games and Nintendo's *Wii Sports* and *Wii Fit* titles. MBVGs, sometimes referred to as "exergames," have not been yet been formally incorporated into esports; however, like esports, they redefine traditional notions of exercise and sport. A meta-analysis of exergaming studies conducted by Gao, Chen, & Pope (2015) concluded that MBVGs[1] can have profound impacts on children's and adolescents' psychological and physiological well-being compared to sedentary activities. They found that playing MBVGs increases heart rate, energy expenditure, metabolic equivalent (oxygen consumed versus calories burned at rest), and maximal oxygen intake during intense exercise.

Esports Injuries

While many may not think that engaging in a relatively sedentary activity like playing video games would result in physical injury, esports players are, in fact, highly susceptible to health concerns tied to chronic overuse – most commonly, hand and wrist injuries (Brautigam, 2016). DiFrancisco-Donoghue, Balentine, Schmidt, & Zwibel (2019) surveyed 65 collegiate esports competitors throughout the United States and Canada and found the most common health complaints to be eye strain (56%), neck and back pain (42%), wrist pain (36%), and hand pain (32%), with only 2% of the sample reporting seeking medical attention. Moreover, 40% reported not engaging in physical exercise. In addition to eye strain from viewing a computer screen for several hours a day of practice and competitions, DiFrancisco-Donoghue et al. (2019) note that players may experience retinal and photoreceptor damage from prolonged exposure to light-emitting diode (LED) lighting. LED exposure can also lower a person's melatonin levels, which can affect the sleep cycles. They suggest esports players take breaks from their computer screens to refocus their eyes.

Unique to esports is the "gamer thumb" – an injury resulting from locking the thumb and trigger finger for extensive amount of time that prevents players from being able to bend their thumb (Gaudiosi, 2018). Levi Harrison, an orthopedic surgeon in Los Angeles specializing in upper body and shoulder injury and hand rehabilitation, has established the United States' first esports-focused medical practice. He also creates YouTube videos educating video game players on stretching, taking appropriate breaks between play sessions, and improving circulation (Gaudiosi, 2018).

Mental Health

Smith, Birch, and Bright (2019) found that esports competitors are subjected to many of the same stressors as traditional sport athletes, from team communication problems to media interviews. One of the biggest health challenges facing esports professionals is mental health – a major culprit being emotional fatigue, or burnout. Between 80 hours of week of practice and the immense pressure to perform in high-stakes situations, players – most of whom are in their teens or early 20s – naturally succumb to what many refer to as "the grind" (Hassan, 2018). Pro Smash Bros. Melee player, Justin "Plup" McGrath, sparked conversation about anxiety among esports players after experiencing his first panic attack on stage at the 2018 EVO fighting tournament. McGrath, the favorite to win the title, ended up placing third overall (Erzberger, 2018).

For many teams that house their players in a "gaming house," which functions as both a residence and training facility, the added stress of living and working in the same environment takes a toll (Reambes, 2018). Hence, it is unsurprising that many among the gaming elite retire by their mid-20s (Gera, 2014). In 2018, Team Liquid and computer manufacturer Alienware partnered to open an 8,000 square foot esports training facility in Los Angeles. While the facility boasts cutting-edge training technology, such as Tobii eye-tracking software, the main agenda, according to Team Liquid and Alienware, is to combat player burnout. Their training facility is the first not to also double as a residence for a team (Reambes, 2018).

While the pressure and "the grind" of esports can certainly be taxing on players, there are also potential mental health benefits to consider. Esports professionals have reported gaining more self-confidence, coping strategies, and stress relief through playing (Sacco, 2017). Learning how to manage stress in high-pressure situations is another valuable skill that players might take away from their experiences (Amirrezvani, 2019). The relatively young age of esports competitors results in many teenagers developing these valuable skills at an earlier age compared to professional athletes in traditional sports.

Recently, more esports teams have begun to emphasize holistic approaches to training, including physical exercise to combat the relatively sedentary hours of practice and competition and yoga and meditation to destress and improve focus (Keh, 2019). While there is little research on the connections between mental health and esports specifically, moderate video game play has been associated with positive mental health outcomes. In a literature review of studies on mental well-being and traditional video game play, Jones Scholes Johnson Katsikitis and Carras (2014) concluded that playing video games – in moderation – can contribute positively to happiness and well-being. Specifically, the literature points to games as therapeutic tools for relaxation and stress reduction.

Conclusion

What was once an activity confined to internet cafes and bedrooms is now a multibillion dollar global spectacle. The rapid expansion of the esports industry is an exciting celebration of elite gaming, and one that continues to push the boundaries of what it means to play and watch video games. Yet with this new era also comes challenges such as regulating esports gambling and managing players' health and well-being. As more high schools and colleges around the world develop their own esports clubs and teams (Dvorak, 2019), the importance of knowledge on esports' effects on players, fans, and society as a whole cannot be overstated.

Note

1 Gao Chen & Pope (2015) refer to them as Active Video Games (AVGs) in their analysis. I use AVGs, MBVGs, and exergaming interchangeably here.

References

Amirrezvani, D. (2019, April 19). Optimising esports performance—Health body, healthy mind. *Esports Insider*. Retrieved from https://esportsinsider.com/2019/04/the-esports-doctor-david-amirrezvani-better-mental-health-really-does-improve-performance.

Andrews, D., & Ritzer, G. (2018). Sport and presumption. *Journal of Consumer Culture*, 18(2), 356–375. doi: 10.1177/1469540517747093.

Braithwaite, B. (2018, August 31). Breaking down the major streaming platforms in esports. *The Esports Observer*. Retrieved from https://esportsobserver.com/breakdown-streaming-platforms.

Brautigam, T. (2016). Esports needs to face its injury problem. *Esports Observer*. Retrieved from https://esportsobserver.com/esports-needs-face-injury-problem.

Caillois, R. (2001). *Man, play, and games*. Urbana, IL: University of Illinois Press.

Carter, M., & Gibbs, M. (2013). eSports in *EVE Online*: Skullduggery, fair play and acceptability in an unbound competition. *Proceedings from the 8th International Conference on the Foundations of Digital Games*, May 14–17, 2013, Chania, Crete, Greece. Retrieved from http://www.fdg2013.org/program/papers.html.

Chalk, A. (2019, January 24). ESL will hold its first-ever Fortnite tournament at IEM Katowice 2019. *PC Gamer*. Retrieved from https://www.pcgamer.com/esl-will-hold-its-first-ever-fortnite-tournament-at-iem-katowice-2019.

Consalvo, M. (2009). *Cheating: Gaining advantage in video games*. Cambridge, MA: MIT Press.

Counter-Strike: Global Offensive. (2012). Bellevue, WA: Valve video game.

Dance Dance Revolution. [Computer software]. (1998). Tokyo: Konami [video game].

DiFrancisco-Donoghue, J., Balentine, J., Schmidt, G., & Zwibel, H. (2019). *BMJ Open Sport & Exercise Medicine*, *5* (1), 1–6. doi: 10.1136/bmjsem-2018-000467.

"DogDog." (2019). *Top Twitch Streamers*. Retrieved from https://toptwitchstreamers.com/.

Defense of the Ancients. streamer/dogdog. Dota 2. [Computer software]. (2013). Bellevue, WA: Valve [video game].

Dvorak, P. (2019, July 22). Coming to a high school near you: The brave new world of esports. *The Washington Post*. Retrieved from https://www.washingtonpost.com/local/coming-to-a-high-school-near-you-the-brave-new-world-of-esports/2019/07/22/331919d2-aca3-11e9-bc5c-e73b603e7f38_story.html.

Ekdahl, D., & Ravn, S. (2018). Embodied involvement in virtual worlds: The case of eSports practitioners. *Sports, Ethics, and Philosophy*, *13*(2), 132–144.

Erzberger, T. (2018, August 24). Mental health issues remain pervasive problem in esports scene. Retrieved from https://www.espn.com/esports/story/_/id/24427802/mental-health-issues-esports-remain-silent-very-real-threat-players.

ESPN. (2019, July 29). And @bugha is only 16 years old! [Tweet text]. Retrieved from https://twitter.com/espn/status/1155893266098872322.

Eve Online. [Computer software]. (2003). New York City: Simon & Schuster Interactive.

FIFA. [Computer software]. (1991). Redwood City, CA: EA Sports.

Fogel, S. (2018, July 11). ESPN, Disney, ABC airing Overwatch League. *Variety*. Retrieved from https://variety.com/2018/gaming/news/espn-disney-abc-overwatch-league-1202870413/.

Gao, Z., Chen, S., & Pope, Z. (2015). A meta-analysis of active video games on health outcomes among children and adolescents. *Obesity Reviews*, *16*(9), 783–794. doi: 10.1111/obr.12287.

Gaudiosi, J. (2018, May 3). As esports grows, so does need for esports doctors. *Variety*. Retrieved from https://variety.com/2018/gaming/features/esports-doctor-1202796749.

Gears of War. [Computer software.] (2006). Redmond, WA: Microsoft Studios [video game].

Gera, E. (2014, August 15). What happens when you're too old to play *League of Legends* professionally? *Polygon*. Retrieved from https://www.polygon.com/2014/8/15/6006211 /league-of-legends-riot-games-esports-age.

Gilbert, B. (2019, March 20). How big is '*Fortnite*'? With nearly 250 million players, it's over two-thirds the size of the US population. *Business Insider*. Retrieved from https://www.businessinsider.com/how-many-people-play-fortnite-2018-11.

Godfrey, C. (2018, July 31). 'It's incredibly widespread': Why eSports has a match-fixing problem. *The Guardian*. Retrieved from https://www.theguardian.com/games/2018/jul/31/its-incredibly-widespread-why-esports-has-a-match-fixing-problem.

Granic, I., Lobel, A., & Engels, C. M. E. R. (2014). The benefits of playing video games. *American Psychologist, 69*(1), 66–79. doi: 10.1037/a0034857.

Grove, C., & Krejcik, A. (2015, August 19). eSports betting: It's real, and bigger than you think. Digital and interactive gaming. *Eilers Research*. Retrieved from https://www.esportsbets.com/wp-content/uploads/2015/09/eSports-Betting-White-Paper-Exec-Summary.pdf.

Guild Wars 2. [Computer software]. (2012). Seongnam, South Korea: NCSoft [video game].

Halo 5: Guardians. [Computer software].(2015). Redmond, WA: Microsoft Studios [video game].

Hardenstein, T. S. (2017). "Skins" in the game: *Counter-Strike*, esports, and the shady world of online gambling. *UNLV Gaming Law Journal, 7*(2). Retrieved from https://scholars.law.unlv.edu/glj/vol7/iss2/.

Hassan, A. (2018, December 27). Esports players are burning out in their 20s. *Quartz at Work*. Retrieved from https://qz.com/work/1509134/esports-players-are-burning-out-in-their-20s-because-of-stress.

Hearthstone. [Computer software]. (2014). Irvine, CA: Blizzard Entertainment [video game].

Heaven, D. (2014, August 13). Esports: Pro video gaming explodes with big prize pots. *New Scientist*. Retrieved from https://www.newscientist.com/article/mg22329823-900-esports-pro-video-gaming-explodes-with-big-prize-pots/#.VR9OzeEyRxI.

Heitner, D. (2018, May 2). A look inside Riot Games, from $320,000 player salaries to using esports as a catalyst for sales. *Forbes*. Retrieved from https://www.forbes.com/sites/darrenheitner/2018/05/02/a-look-inside-riot-games-from-320000-player-salaries-to-using-esports-as-a-catalyst-for-sales/#214f6d972c6a.

Holden, J. T., & Ehrlich, S. C. (2017). Esports, skins betting, and wire fraud vulnerability. *Gaming Law Review, 21*(8): 566–574. 10.1177/1461444818786216.

Jenny, S. E., Hushman, G. F., & Hushman, C. J. (2013). Pre-service teachers' perceptions of motion-based video gaming in physical education. *International Journal of Technology in Teaching and Learning, 9*(1), 98–111. Retrieved from https://eric.ed.gov/?id=EJ1213570.

Jenny, S. E., Manning, R. D., Keiper, M. C., & Olrich, T. W. (2016). Virtual(ly) athletes: Where eSports fit within the definition of "sport." *Quest, 69*(1), 1–18. doi: 10.1080/00336297.2016.1144517.

Jin, D. (2010). ESports and television business in the digital economy. In D. Jin (Ed.), *Korea's online gaming empire* (pp. 59–79). Cambridge, MA: MIT Press.

Jones, C. M., Scholes, L., Johnson, D., Katsikitis, M., & Carras, M. C. (2014). Gaming well: Links between videogames and flourishing mental health. *Frontiers in Psychology, 5*, 260. doi: 10.3389/fpsyg.2014.00260.

Keh, A. (2019, April 2). Esports embraces traditional training methods: Less pizza, more yoga. *The New York Times*. Retrieved from https://www.nytimes.com/2019/04/02/sports/esports-league-of-legends.html.

Khalid, A. (2019, March 25). Philadelphia Fusion will open the first arena US arena built for esports. *Engadget*. Retrieved from https://www.engadget.com/2019/03/25/overwatch-team-philadelphia-fusion-will-open-the-first-esports-arena-in-the-us/.

Kim, Y., & Ross, S. D. (2006). An exploration of motives in sport video gaming. *International Journal of Sports Marketing & Sponsorship, 8*(1), 28–40. doi: 10.1108/IJSMS-08-01-2006-B006.

League of Legends. [Computer software]. (2012). Los Angeles: Riot Games [video game].

Macey, J., & Hamari, J. (2018). Investigating relationships between video gaming, spectating esports, and gambling. *Computers in Human Behavior, 80,* 344–353. doi: 10.1016/j.chb.2017.11.027.

Madden. [Computer software]. (1988). Redwood City, CA: EA Sports [video game].

Meola, A. (2018a, January 9). How esports have given rise to competitive gaming betting and gambling—with skins and real money. *Business Insider.* Retrieved from https://www.businessinsider.com/the-rise-of-esports-betting-and-gambling-2018-1.

Meola, A. (2018b, January 12). The biggest companies sponsoring esports teams and tournaments. *Business Insider.* Retrieved from https://www.businessinsider.com/top-esports-sponsors-gaming-sponsorships-2018-1.

Mickunas, A. (2019, February 4). How does League's Worlds viewership compare to the Super Bowl? *Dot Esports.* Retrieved from https://dotesports.com/league-of-legends/news/league-of-legends-vs-superbowl-viewer-numbers.

Moore, B. (2019, January 31). Overwatch League is finally letting viewers choose their own camera angle. *PC Gamer.* Retrieved from https://www.pcgamer.com/overwatch-league-is-finally-letting-viewers-choose-their-own-camera-angle.

Mortal Kombat. [Computer software]. (1992). Chicago: Midway. [video game].

Mozur, P. (2014, October 19). For South Korea, E-sports is national pastime. *The New York Times.* Retrieved from https://www.nytimes.com/2014/10/20/technology/league-of-legends-south-korea-epicenter-esports.html.

NBA 2K. [Computer software]. (1999). Novato, CA: 2K Games [video game].

Newzoo. (2019). Global esports market report. Retrieved from https://newzoo.com/solutions/standard/market-forecasts/global-esports-market-report/.

Oh, Y., & Yang, S. (2010). Defining exergames and exergaming. *Paper presented at the Meaningful Play 2010 Conference,* October 21–23, 2010, East Lansing, MI. Retrieved from http://meaningfulplay.msu.edu/proceedings2010/mp2010_paper_63.pdf.

Overwatch. [Computer software]. (2016). Irvine, CA: Blizzard Entertainment [video game].

Ozanian, M., Settemi, C., & Perez, M. (2018, October 23). The world's most valuable esports companies. *Forbes.* Retrieved from https://www.forbes.com/sites/mikeozanian/2018/10/23/the-worlds-most-valuable-esports-companies-1/#2200db746a6e.

Patterson, C. (2019, April 25). Average LCS player salary revealed and it's surprisingly high. *Dexerto.* Retrieved from https://www.dexerto.com/league-of-legends/average-lcs-player-salary-revealed-surprisingly-high-575486.

Rambusch, J., Jakobsson, P, & Pargman, D. (2007). Exploring e-sports: A case study of gameplay in *Counter-strike.* In *Proceedings of the 2007 DiGRA International Conference, Situated Play,* September 24–28, Tokyo, Japan. Retrieved from http://www.digra.org/digital-library/forums/4-situated-play.

Reambes, M. (2018, March 23). How Team Liquid's Alienware Facility Aims to Prevent Athlete Burnout. *SportTechie.* Retrieved from https://www.sporttechie.com/team-liquid-alienware-facility-prevent-athlete-burnout-esports/.

Rocket League. [Computer software]. (2015). San Diego, CA: Psyonix [video games].

Sacco, D. (2017, May 14). Let's talk about mental health in esports: 10 individuals share their stories. *Esports News UK.* Retrieved from https://esports-news.co.uk/2017/05/14/esports-mental-health-experiences.

Sarkar, S. (2018, January 12). MLS launching esports league for FIFA 18 World Cup. *Polygon.* Retrieved from https://www.polygon.com/2018/1/12/16880590/fifa-18-esports-world-cup-emls.

Seo, Y., & Jung, S. (2016). Beyond solitary play in computer games: The social practices of eSports. *Journal of Consumer Culture, 16*(3), 635–655. doi: 10.1177/1469540514553711.

Shieber, J. (2019, July 28). Fortnite World Cup has handed out $30 million in prizes, and cemented its spot in the culture. *TechCrunch.* Retrieved from https://techcrunch.com/2019/07/28/fortnite-world-cup-has-handed-out-30-million-in-prizes-and-cemented-its-spot-in-the-culture.

Smith, M. J., Birch, P. D. J., & Bright, D. (2019). Identifying stressors and copying strategies of elite esports competitors. *International Journal of Gaming and Computer-Mediated Simulations, 11*(2). doi: http://dx.doi.org/10.4018/IJGCMS.2019040102.

Stafford, T., & Dewar, M. (2014). Tracing the trajectory of skill learning with a very large sample of online game players. *Psychological Science, 25*(2), 511–518. doi: 10.1177/0956797613511466.

StarCraft. [Computer software] (1998). Irvine, CA: Blizzard Entertainment [video games].

Stubbs, M. (2019, July 27). The International 9 'Dota 2' tournament prize pool breaks $30 million. *Forbes.* Retrieved from https://www.forbes.com/sites/mikestubbs/2019/07/27/the-international-9-dota-2-tournament-prize-pool-breaks-30-million/#7218da2d2c07.

Su, N. M., & Shih, P. C. (2011). Virtual spectating: Hearing beyond the video arcade. *Proceedings from the 25th BCS Conference on Human Computer Interaction,* Newcastle Upon Tyne, July 4–8, 2011, pp. 269–278. Swinton: British Computer Society.

Summers, N. (2019, February 28). Nike embraces esports with 'League of Legends' sponsorship deal. *Engadget.* Retrieved from https://www.engadget.com/2019/02/28/nike-esports-sponsorship-league-legends-lpl-china/?guccounter=1&guce_referrer=aHR0cHM6Ly93d3cuZ29vZ2xlLmNvbS8&guce_referrer_sig=AQAAAEoCBqcygcmGmPAD-kAOEsN_9LLNAFu17OyUkPF1caZXxAp9pioWTo7vpMERrOZhQvfpHOL5KnlOYOogGB_tdiW6E6-INYoHIefFdZks5rLHI0Mngd7s7typPt-L2VFe-5uMz7RzNOCdjBRtfOBSdIkVq2i7UTv97__Lm4E1ovyP.

Taylor, T. L. (2012). *Raising the stakes: Esports and the professionalism of computer gaming.* Cambridge, MA: MIT Press.

Thiborg, J., & Carlsson, B. (2010). Law and morality in *Counter-Strike. Entertainment and Sports Law Journal, 8*(2), 1. doi: http://doi.org/10.16997/eslj.34.

Tom Clancy's Rainbow Six Siege. [Computer software].(2015). Montreuil, France: Ubisoft [video games].

"Top games awarding prize money." (2020). *Esports Earnings.* Retrieved from https://www.esportsearnings.com/games

Toril, P., Reales, J. M., & Ballesteros, S. (2014). Video game training enhances cognition of older adults: A meta-analytic study. Psychology and Aging, 29(3), 706–716. doi: 10.1037/a0037507.

Quake. [Computer software].(1996). New York, NY: GT Interactive [video games].

Watercutter, A. (2019, July 29). 2 million people streamed the Fortnite World Cup. *Wired.* Retrieved from https://www.wired.com/story/fortnite-world-cup-viewership.

Wilding, M. (2019, January 19). Inside the fight to save esports from big-money match fixes. *Wired.* Retrieved from https://www.wired.co.uk/article/esports-betting-match-fixing.

7

THERAPEUTIC USE OF VIDEO GAMES

Anthony Bean

Much of the debates surrounding video games have to do with their potential for unintentional consequences, whether this be on aggression, addiction, or games and learning. However, recently researchers have turned their attention to the ways that games can be actively utilized as tools for change. This chapter addresses one of these shifts and discusses the use of games in therapeutic contexts. Specifically, it will discuss the potential positive impact of the relational experiences that game players can have with their characters through their in-game experiences. Shifting the discussion away from what video games are doing to players and toward what players are doing with video games has opened a new area of interest about the potential use for video games for therapeutic intervention.

Video games have been the number one leisure activity for the past decade (or even longer for some), overtaking other extracurriculars such as reading and listening to music, across a spectrum of ages (Lenhart et al., 2008). Nearly everyone has heard about video games and is, on a basic level, familiar with the different types of video games available. With the younger generations playing for fun, the middle-aged playing for a break or passing time at home or work, and the elderly playing to keep their minds sharp to stave off dementia, video games have become a distinct part of every culture and age range. The evolving state of virtual worlds and video games creates a future where the imagination is the only limitation.

However, since their development, the virtual worlds of games have been actively debated as either exciting or disastrous for the real life of the video game player. For example, video games continue to be portrayed in the media as a "waste of time" and only played by individuals who are considered to be stereotypical lonely, overweight, underachievers, introverted, lazy, and socially inept (Kowert, Griffiths, & Oldmeadow, 2012), despite the fact that these assumptions are factually incorrect (Durkin & Barber, 2002; Kowert, Festl, & Quandt, 2014) and typically purported by older generations who did not grov with video games as rampantly played as they are today (Ferguson, 2015). These kinds of characterizations have motivated a range of research looking in to the more "negative" aspects of game play, such as problematic gaming/video game addiction and negative impact of online gaming on of "real world relationships." In a way, this focus on the negative has superficially condemned the video game playing population and reinforced the negative stereotypes of a gamer as losers, misanthropes, schizoid, having Asperger's, or socially deviant (Kowert, 2016).

As noted above, these one-sided, negative stereotypes of video gamers have little support in the research literature. For example, Durkin and Barber (2002) found no support for the stereotypical negative beliefs about computer video games and concluded that "computer [video] game play is not necessarily a monolithic, moronic, or antisocial imposition on children's lives" (p. 375). Contrary to popular beliefs about digital games, this study found that among a sample of 1,304 American students, playing video games correlated with positive adolescent development. Compared to adolescents that did not play computer games, gamers reported lower levels of depressed mood, lower levels of substance abuse, lower levels of absenteeism from school, lower levels of risky behavior and disobedience, higher levels of family closeness, and higher levels of active engagement in clubs; finally, they exhibited higher grade point averages.

This variability in what gamers actually looks like – how they think, act, and behave – and the potential for positive media effects have opened the door for a new line of discourse, one that has been notably missing from the debates about video game effects: the positive impact of the relational experience that gamers may have with their characters while playing (i.e., their in-game experience). Shifting the discussion away from what video games are doing to players and toward what players are doing with video games has opened a new area of interest about the potential use for video games for therapeutic intervention.

Therapeutic Video Game Play

When video games entered the mainstream, there was a push in research to determine whether they were helpful or a hindrance. Early research into the phenomenon of video games suggested that electronic play led to low motivation and social interactions and could lead to obesity (for an overview of this research, see Kowert, 2015). However, in recent years, researchers have shifted their focus toward the potential benefits of video game play.

For example, there has been a wealth of research noting that video games can help foster various facets of emotional and intellectual development (Granic, Lobel, & Engels, 2013; Kato, 2010; Redd et al., 1987; Turkle, 1994; Vasterling, Jenkins, Tope, & Burish, 1993). Olson (2010) found youth who played video games were better able to express creativity, had increased social and intellectual curiosity, and had a larger focus to discover the real world compared to youth who did not play video games. Video games have also been linked to improved reading and abstract thinking (Gee, 2007; Koster, 2005; Squire & Barab, 2004), pain management (Kato, 2010; Redd et al., 1987; Vasterling, Jenkins, Tope, & Burish, 1993), and increased cooperation and enthusiasm about psychotherapy in mental health treatment (Bean, 2018; Kato, 2010).

Researchers have also noted that online video games may help lower symptoms associated with high anxiety and depression and be helpful for positive self-esteem, social interactions, and social engagement, particularly for players with certain clinical conditions such as autism (Adachi & Willoughby, 2013; Durkin & Barber, 2002; Durkin, 2010; Ringland, Wolf, Faucett, Dombrowski, & Hayes, 2016; Shute, Ventura, & Ke, 2015; Valkenburg & Peter 2011). More specifically, game play has been found to contribute to increased social interactions of individuals who suffer from difficulties with social engagement along with increasing curricular engagement (Adachi & Willoughby, 2013; Durkin, 2010; Shute, Ventura, & Ke, 2015). For instance, games like *Minecraft* may be particularly valuable in promoting social engagement for individuals on the autism spectrum due to its promotion of prosocial behaviors, social engagement and empowerment, and problem solving skills (Adachi & Willoughby, 2013; Ringland, Wolf, Faucett, Dombrowski, & Hayes, 2016).

Video games are effective learning tools and hold the potential to be therapeutic due (at least partially) to their use of virtual reality and fantasy building, building personal cognitive structures and facilitations of emotions, tackling phobias, processing emotional content, and much more (Bateson, 1972; Jones, 2008; Weisberg, 2013; 2015). In order to understand how games can be used therapeutically, there are three key elements to consider: fantasy and make believe, meaningful and emotional experiences, and psychological projection, which are discussed in more detail below.

Fantasy and Make-Believe

Although it can be tempting to dismiss fantasy play as "only a childhood activity," it is important to realize its cognitive and psychosocial benefits throughout the human lifespan (for an overview, see Connell & Dunlap, 2020). For example, pretend play has been found to shape cognitive structures such as symbolic understanding, theory of mind, and counterfactual reasoning (Bateson, 1972; Weisberg, 2013; 2015).

Suspending belief and normal life has a cauterizing effect on difficult situations that arise from general reality (Jones, 2008). Children use these forms of play in order to process their emotional content and later understand an underlying meaning to the difficulties of life. For example, when a child is expressing violence in a form of play in the therapy room, it does not necessarily mean the child is a violent sociopath, but that he or she is processing an experienced event, requiring the clinician to carefully glean an understanding from the symbolic play (Bean, 2018; Jones, 2008). The play serves as a way to process the emotional content in a natural manner and within a safe place, helping to reduce the tension psychically felt by the child. Video games provide these same principles as outlined as play by these theorists. To play video games is to play a game that has established rules of what can be done and what cannot.

At its core, the act of playing video games is *play* and therefore should be examined from the theoretical perspective of play itself. Additionally, video games and video gamers have a culture of their own, which means we should consider the direct experience that games are having upon the players. That is, the act of play needs to be interpreted within a play-sphere and utilized as a tool in which to apply therapeutic potential (e.g., conversation starters, insight building through character development, Jungian shadow work through the narrative storyline, etc.). By diving into the culture of the video game play with the client, the power of fantasy can become reality when the two are broached appropriately together.

This type of ethnographical approach can be used within any setting but is most powerful when used in a therapeutic atmosphere. Clinicians can use their understanding of their client's motivation to engage within digital worlds to build insight and rapport as well as to help foster personal growth.

Meaningful and Emotional Experiences

Video games can elicit meaningful and emotional content via their immersive storylines and the byproduct of playing. They have been shown to be a safe place for video gamers to experience different forms of reality and play gratifying contextual experiences and demands placed upon them, particularly for adolescents who are in the midst of constructing an identity or experiencing an identity crisis, suggesting an important therapeutic benefit (Frome, 2007). For instance, games like Gone Home (2013) can be utilized by clinicians as a basis for exploring non-cisgender identity, increasing empathetic traits, and question the reality surrounding them all within a video game setting (Baker, 2019). These difficult conversations can be bridged by the video game; player; narrative; and therapist who is familiar with the concepts, game mechanics, and storyline.

Through these perceptions, the video gamer creates emotional and meaningful experiences. They are generated, not just by the game itself, but by the player's interaction with the medium. The narrative aspect of the video game is a large and important measure as the storytelling of the video game can lead gamers to grow closer with their characters. With the inception of character development and creation, the video game player can additionally immerse him- or herself in another manner to create their emotional connection to the video game.

Every story, image, and game have an emotional content that on occasion requires some sifting through to find it – but it exists nevertheless. The emotions may be difficult to understand for some not experienced with them (i.e., rage, empathy, happiness) or not even be seen due to a misconception of the storyline or misinterpreting a scene (crying due to happiness). Exploring these emotions in a safe and controlled context is a crucial part of experiencing and understanding life. When people feel rage, they are angry, as if they have to act, as if someone made a personal attack upon them, and feel threatened. Happiness is on the opposite side of rage, a mental or emotional state of well-being described as positive contentment to flourishing joy. How does one know what these states of being are without feeling them? Stories embrace these emotions and show them through facial features, images, actions, and behaviors. Stories dive into the heart of these emotions and difficult states of being, portraying them efficiently and expertly, without whittling down and losing the experience.

Video games have stories that can elicit these same emotions in individuals through the vicarious experiences of the in-game characters. For example, when Aerith Gainsborough (translated into English: Aeris), a beloved character in *Final Fantasy VII* (Square Enix, 1997) is abruptly killed, most players feel astonished because it is completely unforeseen and because of their connection to the character from the beginning of the game until her unexpected death.

The Therapeutic Benefit of Psychological Projection

Conceptually, projection refers to a phenomenon of an individual taking a part of him- or herself and thrusting it upon an external object or person. Usually this happens unconsciously and the individual is not aware of it. The concept is derived from Freud (1916–1917) and Jung (1960) and suggests that everyone projects outward onto one's surroundings in all aspects of life. While this generally seen as a beneficial process, projection can be maladaptive. When one projects into one's surroundings, one additionally meets others' psychic projections that collide with one another. If one is not aware of the projections and cannot reclaim them, then they can lead to difficult interpersonal problems that require support and can cause significant disruption. An example of this would be when someone first meets someone new and has an unnamed emotional feeling for that person; we would call that a projection. These feelings are not just coming from one person but from everyone at the same time as people psychically work to understand who and what is in front of them and how it impacts them individually. If someone is unable to reclaim and recognize their projections of jealousy, anger, or even distaste, then it will create a divide between the persons and become a barrier to any sort of relationship.

While playing a video game, players are often projecting themselves onto their character. This is a symbiotic relationship – a player can take on an avatar's characteristics just as the avatar can take on the player's characteristics. For example, while playing the *Legend of Zelda,* the player may start to feel empowered as Link prevails through in-game challenges, which could then translate to the player feeling more empowered in daily challenges. Part of the reason this happens is because of the symbiotic relationship. That is, because the player also begins to see Link as an extension of him- or herself. Experiencing a sense of control through an avatar in a virtual space becomes representative of the player gaining a sense of control in out-of-game spaces (Daniels, 2020). In this example, Link's storyline drives the player forward (taking on the avatar's perspective), but the player is also aware that the character is being driven directly by his or her actions (taking on the player's drive). Taken together, Lin's narrative starts to become an internal manifestation of one's own life and personality. As the player concludes battles, quests, and storyline, the character – and player – grow stronger and the opportunity of taking back that newfound strength survives when the immersion concludes and the projection is reclaimed. Playing video games can provide the player with growth opportunities that may not otherwise be found in society and offer that important development we all seek in ourselves (Connell & Dunlap, 2020; Madigan, 2020).

Projection is possible because video game avatars provide an object for this process, and the qualities that are inherent in the character can then be extrapolated and used to internally motivate the client. This is particularly the case when the projection is occurring on characters who seem to "survive against all odds." For example, Master Chief of the *Halo* (Microsoft) games is one which exhibits these qualities. The player assumes the role of Master Chief and has to battle against hordes of opponents that easily outnumber him and survive catastrophic events which would normally kill anyone – and in most cases do kill lesser people in the storyline. Isaac Clarke in the *Dead Space* horror series has a similar battle against an undead form of being. Isaac's ability to be resourceful and engage power stations back online while battling literal death coming at him is admirable to anyone willing to uncover his traumatic storyline. Link in *The Legend of Zelda* (Nintendo), an orphan who travels Hyrule, discovers he is the savior of the realm even though throughout his short life he is shunned as an outsider. The projection bonds with these characters seem to be particularly strong, perhaps due to their resourcefulness in the face of adversity, being able to battle back from insurmountable odds, saving yourself, being an outsider, but still having a purpose. These objects are powerful illustrations of what we can do in life if we are able to harness our internal resources appropriately. It just requires the thoughtful eye and ear of the psychologist or mental health expert, and most importantly a willingness to explore the fantasy with the video gamer to discover what these players mean to them. This part of the process requires an analysis of archetypes.

What Are Archetypes?

Simply put, archetypes are images with universal meanings attached to them (Stein, 1998). They are a widely used and beloved way of experiencing and discussing life, but also one of the most difficult ideas or motifs to conceptualize due to the less than tangible existence they represent. The conceptual idea of these psychologically abstract and literal interpretations of our lives is usually associated with Carl Jung (2014) or James Hillman (2004) as the creators and identifiers of these themes.

Archetypes are everywhere yet must be conceptualized from a metaphorical, symbolic, and non-literal approach to be used in therapy and commonplace life.

Archetypes are identified by the similarities in which they are presented. That is, something is considered an archetype when many different people view them as having similar emotions and cognitions, even when events in which they occur are different. For example, a snowflake is symbolic for winter or air conditioning, while the image of a sun means summer or heat. Similarly, blue is collectively considered to identify cold while red signifies hot. Place these pictures on anything and the person viewing them can understand the representation quite simply.

Notably, many archetypes are experienced cross-culturally. This is part of what makes archetypes so powerful and exceptional to direct experience; they are commonly felt and experienced, even in virtual spaces (Bean, 2015; Hillman, 2004; Jung, 2014). These patterns can be seen through historical texts, art, religion, fables, myths, and video game characters. Viewing players' avatar projections from this point of reference highlights the importance of how they have come to be intertwined into everyday life, therapy, and psychology.

Video Games and Archetypes

Video games uniquely allow individuals to symbolically direct and play as the hero. While playing, individuals are able to fully participate in the myth of the hero, not just watch, read, or observe it. It is the *playing* of the video game that becomes an important action for the player as he or she becomes part of the story (Bean, 2018; Connell & Dunlap, 2020). This is what makes video games unique compared to mythological archetypes: video games' conceptualization of archetypes in a literalized visual format rather than relying on the imagination and interpretation of the reader as in literature or a board game.

Video games literalize the archetype played by the video gamer choosing to interact as one of them. The video game character itself becomes a literalized representation of an archetype. The image of the archetype, avatar played, gives it life, but the *playing* of the character gives it meaning (Bean, 2018).

That is, the character is not simply a collection of pixels. By playing as the character, the video gamer brings meaning to the existence of the pixels. As a player, these pixels come to life and start to provide meaning for the created virtual character. Through this interaction, and the overarching storyline of any particular game, individuals create a narrative for the character that may represent internal manifestations of their own personality.

Bean (2018) identified seven different archetypes in video games by thematically evaluating play styles, weapon choices, character abilities, and backstories from over 100 in-game avatars (see Table 7.1). While each video game, and corresponding game world is unique, there are many commonalities of the different virtual archetypes.

The orphan is often discussed as the "blank slate" character. These types of characters often have a minimal backstory and little to no dialogue, which

TABLE 7.1 Archetypes of Virtual Characters (Adapted from Bean, 2018)

Archetype	Description
Orphan	The video game base archetype, essentially a blank slate to be projected upon.
Warrior	Warriors tend to be the leader of the group, jumping into battle, and keeping the focus on them instead of their comrades in melee combat.
Healer	The healer ensures that their friends stay healthy, alive, and inspires them to continue forward through healing spells.
Ranger	Rangers are scouts, pathfinders, bounty hunters, trackers, woodsmen, hunters, and beast masters and tend to use range weapons.
Rogue	Rogues are similar to assassins and spies and rely on surprise attacks, playing in the shadows, stealth capabilities, careful and cunning watching.
Spellcaster	There are many names by which the spellcaster is known: mage, wizard, sorcerer, witch, warlock, magi, sage, and magician and they primarily use spells.
Engineer	Steady, calculating, patient, and methodical. The Engineer is also a tactician of grand scale war combat. They marshal troops to battle attacking hordes.
Athlete	The Athlete is always available for a challenge or playing with another individual to determine who is superior.

provides the player with the greatest possibility of projection as compared to the other archetypes. An example of the orphan archetype can be seen in Link in the *Legend of Zelda* series of games.

The warrior archetype is the traditional leader and/or fighter character in a game. These characters tend to focus on themselves, rather than the group as a whole, and are adept in situations of close combat. One example is Master Chief in the *Halo* series of games.

The Healer archetype is more introversive and reserved. Healers tend to stay focused on others rather than themselves, which can sometimes lead to failing to care for their own needs. The amount of energy and devotion to others can be overwhelming and sometimes goes unnoticed because of their more reserved demeanor. An example of this avatar is Aerith Gainsborough from *Final Fantasy VII*.

The ranger archetype is versatile and relies on speed, agility, and cunning actions to defeat her opponents. Of all the archetypes, rangers are the most adaptable to their environment. Aragorn from the Tolkien series of books (i.e., *Lord of the Rings*) is a prime example of a ranger.

The rogue archetype is those persons that lurk in the shadows and avoid others. They are similar to assassins as they rely on surprise attacks, stealth, and careful planning. An example of this is Altaïr in *Assassin's Creed*.

There are many names by which the spellcaster archetype is known: mage, wizard, sorcerer, witch, warlock, magi, sage, and magician, to name a few. As one can surmise from the name, the primary ability of this archetype is casting spells. These spells can be protective (i.e., buffing), healing, or damaging to oneself and others. An example of a well-known spellcaster would be Merlin.

Steady, calculating, patient, and methodical – this is what the engineer archetype represents. There is not a puzzle that cannot be solved, a challenge overlooked, or an achievement not attempted. These tasks in and of themselves become an engrossing endeavor, with special care being administered within the game to fulfill specific goals. A prime example of this character would be the persona one must take on when playing the *Civilization* series of games.

The primary attribute of the athlete archetype is the competitive video game play. These kinds of players participate in competitive play in order to determine a winner. An example of this would be competitive *Starcraft*, *League of Legends*, and *Hearthstone* players.

It is important to note that these archetypal roles differ in how they relate and function in the virtual world. Each archetype has varying levels of possible projection (the "blank slate" character having the most); however, with each archetype, the therapist can draw parallels to how these roles relate to the personal and psychological struggles.

Through examination of many video games ranging from 8-bit to AAA video games, archetypal commonalities begin to coalesce based on character qualities and circumstances. These characters can then be seen as existing across different video games in different avatar forms but based in the same creational essence. While there is the possibility of many more archetypes being present in video games, currently there are seven main archetypes of play identified, which transform the character into the archetype of the hero through a narratively transformational track called The Seven Paths of Valor (see Figure 7.1).

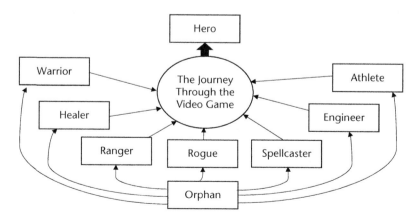

FIGURE 7.1   The Seven Paths of Archetypal Valor (adapted from Bean, 2018)

As seen in Figure 7.1, the Seven Paths of Valor are The Warrior, The Healer, The Ranger, The Rogue, The Spellcaster, The Engineer, and The Athlete. Each of these paths provides a way for the player to experience the "hero's journey" (for more on this, see Connell & Dunlap, 2020) and, through it, become powerful and complete. As players empathize, project, and participate in the avatar's journey, they link their own personal self and history to the character, inherently imprinting upon the character being played. Through the linking of their own personal self and history, the player experiences the same transformation as their character via the storyline becoming consciously and unconsciously healed through the game-play. By utilizing these experiences, players prove to themselves that they can amount to something – they, too, can become a hero.

It is useful to understand the different playable archetypal avatars in video games. This allows a discussion to unfold about the character being played, what is intriguing about it, the game mechanics, powerful emotions and feelings, and behaviors. Categorizing archetypes on the basis of common character qualities allows virtual characters to be seen as existing across different video games in different avatar forms but based on the same creational qualities. These are seven main archetypes of play that transform the character into the archetype of the hero – a powerful being within the virtual landscape and for the client in the clinician's room.

Practical Applications: Video Games as Clinical Tools for Anxiety and Depression

Many video gamers have mood difficulties or a mood disorder that hinders their interpersonal interactions (Bean, 2018). The anxiety becomes too great to handle and leads to a flight response. Depression is overwhelming and leads to avoidance. However, when the video gamer encounters a similar interaction through the choice of video games, the response is different. A clinician can use that/those video game(s) to his or her advantage by taking the game mechanics and over-lapping them into the real world.

For example, some therapists have used *Pokémon Go* (Nintendo) for their social anxiety or depression by playing the video game outdoors and having to walk and also catch the Pokémon (Grohol, 2018). This requires them to interact with others at gyms and Poke stops along their walk path while allowing a safe haven for them to continue on afterwards if their anxiety becomes unmanageable. A tried and true therapeutically inclined manner in which to help with social or general anxiety symptoms is exposure therapy, while interacting and feeling as if one belongs is a tool for depression (Telch, Cobb, & Lancaster; 2014). In essence, exposure therapy focuses upon changing the reaction and response to an object or stimulation that is feared. Through gradual and repetitious exposure, the fear, anxiety, or phobia lessens in strength and allows the individual to learn from the experience. By interacting with other individuals, a person begins to feel as if he or she belongs somewhere, which in turn alleviates isolation and difficulties with social interactions.

Using Pokémon again as an example to exemplify a different approach to anxiety/depression is to make poke balls (which are used to catch Pokémon in the video game) and then have the client catch real life or imaginary objects pretending they are Pokémon. These caught Pokémon can then be used as anxiety/depression moments in which an individual may elicit an anxiety or depression reaction to switch the psyche to thinking they are representing the client's own anxiety. The individual then lets the Pokémon go, which in turn lets his or her anxiety/depression go as well – the individual is symbolically setting the Pokémon/anxiety/depression free. Similarly, the poke ball can be/become a totem for the individuals to ground themselves in moments of difficulty by remembering how they caught and released the anxiety/depression back into the wild.

Teaching the Pokémon different moves within the game is also a way to help with real-life anxiety/depression. In order for the Pokémon to become stronger, an individual has to evolve and learn new moves, increasing his or her statistics while dueling other Pokémon. Using these same principles metaphorically, one can imagine clients as Pokémon trainers and their anxiety/depression as a Pokémon. They, as the trainer, have to then teach and train their Pokémon to harness their own power to relieve the anxiety/depression experiences, thus teaching the trainers how to work with their own difficulties as well. Creating a storyline for their Pokémon additionally is another important and useful component of the game that can be used to tell a story about the client him- or herself, effectively rewriting a difficult portion of anxiety/depression experiences.

Another interesting component of Pokémon is that players gravitate toward specific Pokémon as their favorites. They tend to choose six to twelve out of the hundreds available to be their main Pokémon. By exploring the choice of preferred Pokémon, one can learn more about the personality and self-concept of the individual playing the game, therefore unlocking new knowledge about the person and why he or she makes specific choices within the video game.

While Pokémon was primarily used as an example of how to effectively use the game storyline for understanding and overcoming mood disorders, anxiety, and depression, every video game has a comparable manner in which to be similarly utilized. A therapist needs to be familiar with the virtual realm being played and the mechanics of the realm to bring about these different abilities. Once acquainted with the games, creating these tools becomes much easier and quicker to comprehend.

There are several other examples: Link in *The Legend of Zelda* is an orphan and must overcome his own loss of family to become the hero of Hyrule. This game is particularly good for clients who are adopted or feel abandoned, helping them to see their own personal worth and power. In *World of Warcraft* (Blizzard), players chooses their own identity and character traits, which can be explored further to understand the self-concept and personality of the player. Within games like *Risk* and *Civilization*, there are choices to be made while overcoming the rest of the world and monuments to be built, which increase abilities as well. Exploring these choices further with different gameplay styles is effective for understanding the individual. Every virtual world has the ability to manage and create potential for change. The key for therapists is to be curious about the archetypal draw to the game and how it can be harnessed for interventions. By thinking of the game as a tool in which to understand the video game player, endless possibilities arise for use across environments.

Killing Our Own Monsters

Playing video games has the ability to help conquer our own fears by defeating the monsters within the video games. When first entering a boss or minion fight, the music changes to more rapid and higher pitched tones, exciting the players and causing them to focus into the game further. The beginning of each altercation can be a bit of a scary situation because one does not know what to expect. All of the senses are constantly feeding information to the player as he or she is attempting to figure out how to defeat the boss. The boss looms ahead and causes a sense of fear – a fear of the unknown of what will happen or how to defeat this conundrum ahead of the player.

The relationship, and the defeating of the fear concepts, can be extrapolated from the video game into real life using the same variables the player used to develop their character to appropriately handle their difficulties. With the experience of defeating a monster, it creates an opportunity to use the same processes in which to handle life experiences. Using these concepts in this manner changes the psychological dynamic of the problem being experienced by removing the personal mental obstacle originally created by the video gamer. Utilizing the character's power and trying different tactics to defeat the boss is a form of problem solving, and it takes the player out of a state of freeze and flight while putting him or her into a positive place of fight or courage to handle the situation.

The use of games in therapeutic settings is a growing one, and the aim of this chapter was to highlight the ways that games can provide meaningful experiences and foster learning that can be carried over into other life experiences. Video games are far more than just a fun, frivolous way to pass the time. They are powerful tools for teaching tool for coping, developmental, and social skills in and out of the virtual world.

References

Adachi, P. J. C., & Willoughby, T. (2013). More than just fun and games: The longitudinal relationships between strategic video games, self-reported problem solving skills, and academic grades. *Journal of Youth and Adolescence*, 42(7), 1041–1052.

Baker, L. (2019). Therapy in the digital age. In J. Stone (Ed.), *Integrating technology into modern therapies: A clinician's guide to developments and interventions* (1st ed., pp. 37–47). New York, NY: Taylor & Francis Group.

Bateson, G. (1972). *A theory of play and fantasy: Steps to an ecology of mind.* Chicago, IL: University of Chicago Press.

Bean, A. (2015). Video gamers' personas: A five factor study exploring personality elements of the video gamer. Retrieved from ProQuest Digital Dissertations. (AAT 3726481).

Bean, A. M. (2018). *Working with video gamers and games in therapy: A clinician's guide.* New York, NY: Routledge.

Connell, M., & Dunlap, K. (2020). You are the one Foretold; finding yourself through the journey. In R. Kowert (Ed), *Video games and well-being: Press start.* New York: Palgrave.

Durkin, K. (2010). Videogames and young people with developmental disorders. *Review of General Psychology, 14*(2), 122–140. doi: 10.1037/a0019438.

Durkin, K., & Barber, B. (2002). Not so doomed: Computer game play and positive adolescent development. *Journal of Applied Developmental Psychology, 23*(4), 373–392.

Ferguson, C. J. (2015). Clinicians' attitudes toward video games vary as a function of age, gender and negative beliefs about youth: A sociology of media research approach. *Computers in Human Behavior, 52*, 379–386. Retrieved from https://doi.org/10.1016/j.chb.2015.06.016.

Freud, S. (1916–1917). *Introductory lectures on psycho-analysis.* Standard Edition, 15,16.

Frome, J. (2007). *Eight ways videogames generate emotion.* Proceedings of the 2007 DiGRA International Conference, Tokyo. Retrieved from http://www.digra.org/digital-library/publications/eight-ways-videogames-generate-emotion/.

Gee, J. P. (2007). *Good video games plus good learning.* New York, NY: Peter Lang.

Granic, I., Lobel, A., & Engels, R. C. M. E. (2013). The benefits of playing video games. *American Psychologist, 69*(1), 1–13.

Gone Home. (2013). Unity [video game].

Grohol, J. M. (2018). *Pokémon Go reportedly helping people's mental health, depression.* Retrieved from https://psychcentral.com/blog/pokemon-go-reportedly-helping-peoples-mental-health-depression/.

Hillman, J. (2004). *Uniform edition: 1.* Putnam: Spring Publications.

Jones, G. (2008). *Killing monsters: Why children need fantasy, super heroes, and make-believe violence.* Basic Books.

Jung, C. G. (1960). *The structure and dynamics of the psyche.* Collected works: Vol. 8. Trans. R.F.C. Hull. Princeton: Princeton University Press.

Jung, C. G. (2014). *The archetypes and the collective unconscious.* London: Routledge.

Jung, C. G., & Hull, R. F. C. (2006). *The archetypes and the collective unconscious.* London: Routledge.

Kato, P. M. (2010). Video games in health care: Closing the gap. *Review of General Psychology, 14*(2), 113–121.

Koster, R. (2005). *A theory of fun for game design.* Scottsdale, AZ: Paraglyph Press.

Kowert, R., Griffiths, M., & Oldmeadow, J. A. (2012). Geek or Chic? Emerging Stereotypes of Online Gamers. *Bulletin of Science, Technology, and Society, 32*(6), 471–479.

Kowert, R. (2015). *Video games and social competence.* New York: Routledge.

Kowert, R. (2016). *A parent's guide to video games: The essential guide to understanding how video games impact your child's physical, social, and psychological well-being.* North Charleston, SC: CreateSpace Independent Publishing Platform.

Kowert, R., Festl, R., & Quandt, T. (2014). Unpopular, overweight, and socially inept: Reconsidering the stereotype of online gamers. *Cyberpsychology, Behavior and Social Networking, 17*(3), 141–146. Retrieved from https://doi.org/10.1089/cyber.2013.0118.

Kowert, R., Griffiths, M., & Oldmeadow, J. A. (2012). Geek or Chic? Emerging Stereotypes of Online Gamers. *Bulletin of Science, Technology, and Society, 32,* 471–479. doi: 10.1177/0270467612469078.

Lenhart, A., Kahne, J., Middaugh, E., Rankin Macgill, A., Evans, C., & Vitak, J. (2008). *Teens, video games, and civics: Teens' gaming experiences are diverse and include significant social interaction and civic engagement.* Washington, DC: Pew Internet & American Life Project.

Olson, C. K. (2010). Children's motivations for video game play in the context of normal development. *Review of General Psychology, 14,* 180–187.

Squire, K., & Barab, S. A. (2004). *Replaying history: Learning world history through playing Civilization III.* Indiana University Bloomington. Retrieved from http://website. education.wisc.edu/kdsquire/REPLAYING%20HISTORY.doc.

Stein, M. (1998). *Jung's map of the soul: An introduction.* Chicago: Open Court.

Redd, W. H., Jacobsen, P. B., DieTrill, M., Dermatis, H., McEvoy, M., & Holland, J. C. (1987). Cognitive–attentional distraction in the control of conditioned nausea in pediatric cancer patients receiving chemotherapy. *Journal of Consulting and Clinical Psychology, 55,* 391–395.

Ringland, K. E., Wolf, C. T., Faucett, H., Dombrowski, L., & Hayes, G. (2016) "Will I always be not social?": Re-conceptualizing sociality in the context of a Minecraft community for autism. Proceedings of ACM CHI Conference on Human Factors in Computing Systems, 1256–1269.

Shute, V. J., Ventura, M., & Ke, F. (2015). The power of play: The effects of Portal 2 and Lumosity on cognitive and noncognitive skills. *Computers & Education, 80,* 4, 58–67.

Square Enix (1997). *Final Fantasy VII. [video game].*

Telch, M. J., Cobb, A. R., & Lancaster, C. L. (2014). *Exposure therapy,* vol. 2, 715–756. Bottom of Form.

Turkle, S. (1994). Constructions and reconstructions of self in virtual reality: Playing in the MUDs. *Mind, Culture, and Activity, 1*(3), 158–167.

Valkenburg, P. M. & Peter, J. (2011). Online communication among adolescents: An integrated model of its attraction, opportunities, and risks. *Journal of Adolescent Health, 48*(2), 121–127.

Vasterling, J., Jenkins, R. A., Tope, D. M., & Burish, T. G. (1993). Cognitive distraction and relaxation training for the control of side effects due to cancer chemotherapy. *Journal of Behavioral Medicine, 16,* 65–79.

Weisberg D. S. (2013) Distinguishing imagination from reality. In Taylor M. (Ed.), *The Oxford handbook of the development of imagination.* New York: Oxford University Press; 75–93.

Weisberg, D. S. (2015). Pretend play. *Wiley Interdisciplinary Reviews. Cognitive Science, 6,* 3.

8

EXTENDED REALITY THERAPY

The Use of Virtual, Augmented, and Mixed Reality in Mental Health Treatment

Jessica Stone

Virtual reality (VR), augmented reality (AR), and mixed reality (MR) are all included under the extended reality (XR) umbrella. These powerful platforms include immersive and integrative experiences that can enhance and expand mental health treatment in many ways. This chapter will explore clinical uses and concerns regarding the therapeutic use of XR, alongside the contextual history regarding its development. Therapist comfort and competence are of utmost importance when utilizing therapeutic XR and are discussed in terms of education, experience, and clinical supervision. The integration of XR into modern therapeutic practice is an exciting and powerful addition to a therapist's clinical repertoire.

Advancements in immersive technology have benefited many fields. A natural extension of the amazingly popular use of video games, for both personal and professional reasons, is the use of virtual reality and its exciting cousins, augmented and mixed reality. The immersive nature of these newly popular media allows the user to interact, create, choose, explore, and play in spine-tingling ways. Inclusion in mental health treatment opens the doors to the possibilities of moving beyond describing, orchestrating, and imagining to experiencing that which is therapeutic in ways that engage the polyvagal, autonomic, sympathetic, and parasympathetic systems. In essence, this is a truly a whole-body experience.

Other professional disciplines that have embraced these media are quite varied and include many critical aspects of our society. This extension of the video game family has broadened the scope of effectiveness for these important computer-generated tools. Virtual reality headsets and tablets are now used to aid pediatric medical procedures (Burns-Nader, 2019), assist low vision patients (Deemer et. al., 2019), and provide various forms of medical training (Jin et al., 2017). Virtual reality is also commonly used for flight simulation for pilots (Ellis, 2018), military training of various types (Presnall, 2019; Stone, 2017; Szoldra, 2018), and occupational training for those re-entering society after prison (Clarke, 2019).

The use of extended reality (XR; includes virtual, augmented, and mixed reality, which are discussed in more detail below) in professional training has grown in the last few years, with early reports indicating its effectiveness. For example, when researchers compared learning retention between a group who was instructed via watching a video and a group who learned from a virtual instructor using virtual reality (VR), the VR group demonstrated a 25% increase in accuracy of recall (Bailenson, 2018). These researchers concluded that results indicate "people learn better by doing than by watching ... those who learn best are simulating motor action in the brain" (Bailenson, 2018, p. 39).

The mental health field, in particular, can benefit from adaptation of the appropriate use of digital tools for direct client services. While mental health professionals have been slower to adopt the use of technology in professional ways, there are programs that have been developed for use in therapeutic sessions (Baker, 2019; Lamb & Etopio, 2019; Stone, 2019) and for working with special populations such as veterans (Rizzo & Shilling, 2017) and those on the autism spectrum (Bellani et al., 2011). Using XR within a variety of mental health therapies broadens the scope of treatment, expands services to a wider audience, and can greatly reduce the cost of treatment. This chapter will focus on the introduction of the use of XR hardware and software in mental health treatment. Special focus will be placed on the importance of therapist comfort and competence to expand mental health treatment and benefit people of all cultures, orientations, lifestyles, and needs (Stone, 2019).

The Next Revolution Is Here

It was predicted that 2020 will be a tipping point for gaming. It is likely that more people will have played video games than those who have not (Milijic, 2019). This claim can be supported by the rise of the digital native (Prensky, 2001) and the estimated 2.6 billion gamers worldwide (Andre, 2020). People who enjoy video games, on a plethora of available platforms, have become the norm and not the outlier. Gaming platforms are also an entry point to virtual reality for many users. Indeed, it is predicted that 171 million people will use virtual reality technology in 2020 (Milijic, 2019), so this is developing into a mass market. The inclusion of such tools in therapeutic settings is a natural progression. Today, there are many different interactions of "extended reality," including virtual, augmented, and mixed reality.

Extended Reality (XR)

Extended reality comprises virtual, augmented, and mixed reality. This variety of available gaming hardware and software offers numerous options for casual and professional use. For the purpose of this chapter, a brief overview of current XR components will be presented.

Virtual Reality (VR)

Virtual reality refers to fully immersive experiences, including a 360-degree view of video with real-world content, computer-generated content, or a combination of both (Irvine, 2017). VR uses computers and hardware in a way that "eliminate[s] the traditional separation between user and machine, providing more direct and intuitive interaction with information" (Bricken & Byrne, 1993, p. 200). The sensors track body, head, and hand movements in ways that reflect natural movements, allowing for a sense of immersion and congruency (Maples-Keller et al., 2017; Stone, 2020).

Virtual reality is typically experienced through a headset called a "head-mounted display," or hmd. Historically used in research, academia, and various industry laboratories, an important progression from the 1960s to now has allowed for mass-consumer access and use. Bulky, expensive, uncomfortable units with minimal immersion have given way to lighter, smaller, immersive hmds (Brooks, 1999; Mandal, 2013; Stone, 2020). Palmer Luckey, mentored by Mark Bolas and others, ignited this new era of VR with a hmd driven by a personal computer (Beilinson, 2014; Dudley, 2018; Rubin, 2014).

Once the VR head-mounted display (VR-hmd) is worn, the person is transported to that location or scenario and multiple senses are engaged. As an example, when a VR world depicts a height, everything in that person's body is telling them that they are actually at that height and fear arousal and responses can ensue. Many people will have their autonomic nervous system activated and will begin to sweat, have a sinking feeling in their stomach, have increased heart rate, and more. These responses indicate that the user is immersed and interacting with the environment with his or her senses and potentially more, depending on the program used.

Augmented Reality (AR)

Augmented reality includes computer-generated content depicted as an overlay (appears as a layer over the real-world material) of the physical world environment. This computer-generated content does not interact with the environment (Stone, 2020). For example, clients could overlay a model of another person they want to interact with into the physical space they are currently in. This could allow the client to interact with the person and role play difficult conversations or share content with a loved one who had died. With AR, the overlay would be less complex (the character sits or stands motionless as they would in a static picture) as compared with mixed reality.

Mixed Reality (MR)

Mixed reality has the ability for computer-generated objects to interact with the environment, often referred to as occlusion (Irvine, 2017; Stone, 2020).

TABLE 8.1 Extended, virtual, augmented, and mixed reality (Adopted From Irvine, 2017)

Reality type	Description
Virtual reality (VR)	Immersive experiences real-world content (360-degree video) computer-generated or both
Augmented reality (AR)	Overlay of computer-generated content on the physical real world
Mixed reality (MR)	Overlay of computer-generated content incorporates occlusion
Extended reality (XR)	Incorporates all aspects of VR, AR, and MR

Returning to the example of the client and loved one example: in MR the loved one could move behind a real-world plant or sit on a chair, whereas in AR the loved one would simply be superimposed in front of the plant. This important occlusion feature has a higher level of interactivity between the computer-generated object and the physical real-world environment. Regarding MR and AR, Irvine (2017) offers the following: "The general distinction is: all MR is AR, but not all AR is MR. AR is a composite. MR is interactive." (Irvine, 2017, para 12; Stone, 2020). Although Dudley (2018) states that some people are predicting that the benefit of AR and MR is that the user does not need to be "sealed off in self-contained artificial environments" (para 6), it is also possible that VR allows for the immersion and flow necessary to elicit a therapeutic process due to the sealed off environment, thus creating a completely different world (Stone, 2020). For an overview of the different components of XR, see Table 8.1.

While VR typically gets the most attention when discussing XR, there is a lot of informal discussion among pro fessionals happening currently regarding the use of AR and MR in a psychological and medical treatments. Both AR and MR have the potential to allow clients in a mental health setting to overlay a scene or character onto the existing environment (i.e., one's living room, the therapist's office, etc.). The therapeutic benefits of applying customized, personalized content overlaid into the physical environment are far reaching. For example, firefighters are reportedly using it to see structures and more in thick smoke and to more easily communicate with a base (Bell, 2017).

Within the field of psychology, XR provides considerable flexibility as the therapist can choose from multiple hardware options and gain considerable control over the therapeutic environment. Specific experiences are only limited by the programs available, and the options are expanding daily. The therapist can titrate the exposure for the client and customize the experience. The client can control his/her involvement both within the programs through choices made and also outside of the program by removing the headset at any time. For example, historically, *in-vivo* exposure therapy has had many logistic and financial limitations.

With XR, a client can experience the same kind of exposure therapy with increased environmental and experiential control (Wilson & Soranzo, 2015) and at a much lower time and monetary cost. As discussed by Maples-Keller and colleagues (2017), "[XR] allows for controlled delivery of sensory stimulation via the therapist, is a convenient and cost-effective treatment." (p. 103).

XR in Therapeutic Treatment

With the advent of any new technology, there are apprehensions about the uses and effects in general and within the mental health field. The use of XR in mental health treatment has been no different. While some clinicians see it as a new opportunity to enhance and modify pre-existing treatments, as well as develop new ones, others see it as potentially reckless and non-therapeutic. Some of the primary debates relate to therapist competence and therapeutic interaction concerns.

Therapist Competence

One of the primary concerns is how implementation of XR in mental health will be impacted by therapist competence. In this context, competence refers to the education, supervision, and experience of the clinician. Each of these is critical for fulfilling professional and ethical requirements. If a clinician does not understand the XR being used, or why it is being integrated, how will the assessment, intervention, and integration phases of the therapeutic process be successful? Ethical considerations regarding competence must be addressed. This applies to any medium or clinical process and certainly with the use of XR as it is relatively new to the mental health clinician's repertoire.

Of all the concerns, these are perhaps the easiest to alleviate as education for the use of XR is available in the form of books, videos, and training seminars. Personal play and experience are key for understanding which components are therapeutic; which software will best assist clients with particular concerns; and what each program might "pull for" in terms of coping skills, interactive abilities, nurturing, frustration tolerance, strategic processes, and much more (Stone, 2016, 2019, 2020). Clients will respond positively and have more confidence in the intervention when the therapist has confidence in and knowledge about the programs. Therapists' competence also directly impacts their ability to explain the use of the XR programs to caregivers and collateral contacts, which is a key component of the therapeutic process.

Therapeutic Interaction

An important question then becomes how does the use of such tools in therapeutic settings change our interaction with the game environment, the characters, and possibly other participants and even our own self-perception? The more thorough responses to these questions lie in the need for further research.

However, having used VR and AR therapeutically, the anecdotal responses are as follows: (1) the use of XR tools in therapeutic settings changes our interaction with the game environment immensely as the client is now in direct interaction with the world and environment. This experience sets a potentially near-perfect stage for catharsis and abreaction. (2) The interaction with the characters and/or other participants allows for decisions about interaction styles and character development choices in a more direct way than through a board game or monitor; there is an increased experience of cause and effect. (3) Our own self-perception and development are shaped by our environment and our interactions. XR tools allow for a more thorough exploration of one's self, what is important, what is not, what choices are made and why, what the effect of any and all will be – all within a safe environment that can be escaped or exchanged by the control of the client. What happens in the XR world literally stays in the XR world until integration and implementation occurs outside of the XR world. The therapist interacts during the XR use and then utilizes the clinical components outside of the XR world to assist with integration and implementation.

Integration and implementation are other critical areas within the clinical process. The clinician is there to guide the client through and witness the components of the experience while incorporating each into the treatment plan and goals. Applying the experiences to the client's real-world needs will assist with generalizing what has been gained through the XR use. These are all components that separate personal from professional use.

Case Illustrations

Case illustrations are presented in this chapter to highlight and demonstrate the therapeutic powers of using XR in mental health treatment. A variety of client ages and concerns are provided to illustrate the utility and versatility of these tools. XR has the potential to provide mental health treatment in unique, specific, immersive, and integrated ways.

Case Study: Meditation Programs

Melissa is a 32-year-old woman who has been in weekly psychological outpatient treatment for approximately five months. She initially presented for treatment due to the effects of her loss and abandonment history, which included a high level of anxiety mixed with depression. She has had social and familial difficulties; interpersonal relationships and interactions have been difficult for her over time.

Over the course of treatment, she progressed well in certain areas, such as more ease and trust in interpersonal relationships, social interaction improvement, fewer depressive symptoms, and less difficulties at home. However, her anxiety had remained at an undesired level. Attempts to identify coping skills and strategies that worked well for her were met with little insight and/or hefty resistance. It was clear that a highly motivating, novel experience was needed to make another attempt at identifying what she defined as safe, relaxing, and perceived lowered anxiety. It was decided that virtual reality would be introduced into the treatment. Prior to the introduction, a discussion regarding treatment progress to date and the rationale behind incorporating VR into the treatment took place. Consent was obtained and treatment continued.

Melissa was very interested in virtual reality. She had a personal headset she could use with her phone but had never used a more sophisticated head mounted display unit, which in this case was the HTC Vive. She was initially oriented to the controllers and was seated in the center of a rug for the initial use. The office area rug is a useful parameter in this room as stepping off the rug is a sensation one can register without sight and can keep the user away from stationary objects such as walls, doors, and furniture. Having her begin seated allowed her to acclimate to the headset and controllers at her own pace.

Initially she was introduced to a program called *theBlu*. This program is available through Steam and has three areas to explore. One area has reefs, turtles, manta rays, fish, jellyfish, and a colorful landscape. A second area is a shipwreck scene that includes sea life and a large whale that comes over to look at the player, and the third is a deep sea experience that is dark and initially requires the use of a flashlight through the controller. Melissa started with the first option, the turtle and jellyfish experience. If she had chosen the deep sea option initially, I would have strongly suggested she begin with a different option and then worked to the deep sea. I did not want her to begin with a dark scenario, especially since we were there to work on her anxiety. It would be a great experience to work toward, but not begin with.

Melissa sat on the floor in the office expressing great delight at the scene and creatures she was experiencing. She reached over at her own discretion to touch different plant life and animals. The haptic response in the controller allowed her to feel as though she were actually touching something, along with the visual representation and responsiveness of the three-dimensional computer-generated sea creature. For example, when she tapped the sea anemones, they closed up like colorful flowers retreating into their own shells, and the jellyfish had temporary indents in their bodies and moved backward in response to her touch.

Soon Melissa was ready to move to the whale experience. The whale comes close to the user and at one point the whale's eye is level to the user's eye. As a precaution, the therapist informed her of this in advance, with the intention of front loading any portions that may have raised her anxiety. She was also informed that she could remove the hmd at any time. A careful and continuous evaluation of Melissa's body language, spoken language, and observable biomarkers was important to determine if the intervention was appropriate.

Melissa enjoyed the first two sea experiences and opted not to try the third (deep sea). In an effort to identify what kinds of environments felt peaceful and anxiety reducing, the program *Nature Treks* was introduced. The controller options for this program are more complex than *theBlu*. The increased complexity titration is important for some users. This, along with beginning in a sitting position, can also decrease the occurrence of simulation sickness. After a brief introduction to the new program, Melissa was ready and excited to begin.

Initially the user in *Nature Treks* is presented with a number of panels that represent different types of environments in nature. Each world has different colors; features; lighting; animals; landscape; topographical components; and, in many, areas of water. Melissa was prompted to choose a panel that she believed represented a calming, peaceful world. She chose the green meadow area. In this program, there are orbs that can allow the user to customize the world in certain ways. After exploring the orbs and understanding that some will allow her to place trees, bushes, rocks, butterflies, and more, she was asked to transport to an area in the program that felt the most peaceful. She identified the area, built up a wall of trees and rocks around herself, changed the lighting to a darker hue, and laid down on the floor. What she was experiencing was that she was truly lying in a meadow of grass, surrounded by sounds of the natural scene as provided by the program and enclosed by her protective measures. In the office, she was laying in the middle of the rug, breathing noticeably more calmly, body language relaxed, and without speaking.

After almost ten minutes, it was time to have her "return" to the office and remove the headset so she could acclimate, if needed, to the reality outside of the program. Approaching her carefully, I prompted her to remove the headset and controllers and she sat up on the floor. She was asked a few questions, including how long she felt she was laying in the meadow. She responded that it was a "minute or two." She was shocked to learn that it was a solid ten minutes before she returned to the office. She reflected the calm and peacefulness of the experience and the environment and that she hasn't felt that way in a very long time. Further identification of ways to self-calm were important and successful portions of therapy in subsequent sessions.

Case Study: Commercially Available Game Program

Isabelle is a 9-year-old third grade student who was referred to therapeutic treatment following a disruptive move and separation from her motherffig. She was moved to another state and lives with her grandparents who are now acting as her primary caregivers. She is an only child and moved to an area where she has no social structure or relationships in place.

Her environment prior to the move was chaotic and disheveled. She had very little parameters or expectations of her except that she would behave in a classic "children should be seen and not heard" manner. Her new environment was more accepting of some typical child behaviors but also had very strict rules and parameters. This was a difficult transition for Isabelle. It was as though her environments were polar opposite in each element: one was permissive as long as she was not noisy or obtrusive, and the other was strict but allowed for her to have a known presence in the home.

Her play prior to the use of VR was very restrictive and "people pleasing." She would not endorse or exhibit any behaviors that could be categorized as anything other than pleasant and quiet. Her affective range was very limited and not congruent with her described historical experiences. Virtual reality was introduced as a way to be in a world without consequences in the "real" world, a place where she could be Isabelle without any effects in her day-to-day experience. This is often achieved in play therapy without VR, but in Isabelle's case, the additional extension of the virtual world shifted her drastically.

After the introduction to VR, the controllers, the room and rug parameters, and initial more simplistic-to-interact-with programs, Isabelle chose to play *Job Simulator*. In this cartoon-like world, the user chooses a work environment and has a floating computer monitor employer who instructs the user through tasks and features. Isabelle used this environment to act out and destroy anything and everything she could find. She threw items all over the office, poured liquid on the electronics, threw items at the boss and over to coworker's cubbies, and ate all sorts of food and left the wrappers all over the place. In this world she did not feel confined to the rules she felt in her typical day-to-day life. She was able to rebel in a safe environment, and she enjoyed it immensely. When asked how she felt in this experience she replied, "free." She continued to use the *Job Simulator* program in session for many weeks. Over time it was observed that she began to destroy but then clean up her environment. Ultimately, she was not destroying, and she paid more attention to what the boss's tasks were. She began to enjoy completing the tasks and moving on to more complicated ones.

During these sessions, a few meetings with the family included discussions about her environments, her transitions, what she was expressing, and her needs. Individual sessions included both the play and some conversations about her experience in the virtual world, what she could do in there that she couldn't in her day to day environment, and any progression her family unit was making after the family therapy discussions. Ultimately, her ability to break through the perceived (within therapy) and realistic (in her home life) confines of the rules she had to live by was successfully facilitated by the use of virtual reality.

Case Study: Virtual Sandtray®

Stephen was a 14-year-old eighth grade student who was referred for difficulties at home and school. He primarily had difficulties with anyone in a position of authority and would choose to suffer dire consequences instead of taking personal responsibility for almost anything, even when confronted with clear evidence. He had been expelled from numerous schools and was causing great disruption in his family, where he was the oldest brother of one male and one female sibling.

For the most part, attempts to discuss scenarios; interactions; and the abcs of behavior (**a**ntecedent, **b**ehavior, **c**onsequence) were unsuccessful. The discussions were predominately circular, with the ultimate conclusion of Stephen externalizing all negative attributes and internalizing/personalizing all positives. He employed polarized "black and white" thinking in most, if not all, scenarios.

Stephen was of above average intelligence and could easily manipulate most situations. He attempted to direct the conversation within session to the point that the therapeutic progression was often stalled. In an effort to utilize a projective technique, but in a fun and engaging way, the *Virtual Sandtray-VR (VSA-VR)* program was introduced. This program expands the time honored projective tool of traditional sandtray therapy. Users can dig, build up, and paint the sand, place and manipulate 3D models, change the skybox (background sky area of the screen), and the liquid layer. The result is a custom world created by the client that can be looked down upon from above or interacted with by walking around on the sand level. The projective nature of the technique is intended to allow the more subconscious beliefs, concerns, and processes to be projected onto the medium, in this case the virtual sandtray world.

Within the *VSA-VR* program, Stephen was able to create a few distinct areas of the tray. He painted the sand in sections; one with grass, one with cobblestone, one with lava. Two of his worlds were incongruent. The scene depicted on the sand's surface were aggressive in a subtle way. The people were interacting in a somewhat benign manner, such as appearing to be in conversation, but then there would be a relatively large spider lurking behind. The grass may have been green, but the liquid below was lava. The cobblestone had a pleasant house placed on it, but the backyard was full of dead trees and animal skulls. The lava area was more overt and dominated by scary figures, zombie creatures, and broken buildings.

Stephen appeared to have a positive experience building his world. He enjoyed the animation of certain models and enjoyed maneuvering the controls to move about the tray and change the angles for the field of vision. Having items hidden and lurking behind others delighted him. When he declared that he was done with the scene, he began telling about it and escorting the therapist through the creation.

He enjoyed pointing out the areas that "seemed" a certain way on the surface but "really weren't" that way at all. Ultimately, it became apparent in his tray and his discussion of the tray that there was a lot of deception happening in his life. He was demonstrating it in the tray and in his day-to-day reality but had not put words to it before. Creating, walking around in, interacting with, and explaining the tray illustrated key concepts that were reflected in how he felt he fit in the world, society, and his family. His view was one of distrust and manipulation, of certain aspects being put forth but not congruent with the underlying dynamics. After further individual sessions of revisiting the tray and concepts, a family session was called and some very frank discussions ensued.

For Stephen, it was a stated relief for him to finally be seen and heard, despite all his outward efforts to the contrary. The *VSA-VR* program allowed him to depict his dynamics in a safe, nonthreatening, nonjudgmental environment. Once it was created, he was so excited about the features that his description happened spontaneously and the dynamics were revealed. The use of this VR program was instrumental in creating the space within which to create the world that depicted his experience in life.

Conclusion

Augmented reality, mixed reality, and virtual reality are all included under the extended reality umbrella and include immersive and integrative experiences that will enhance and expand mental health treatment in many ways. Personal development, coping and interpersonal skills, catharsis, abreaction, and much more through the use of XR can be explored, identified, practiced, and integrated into day-to-day life. Therapist comfort and competence are of utmost importance. Future research should focus on the multitude of factors involved in these interventions and strive for clean and powerful constructs to support the expansion of mental health treatment through the use of XR tools.

References

Andre, L. (2020). *Number of gamers worldwide*. https://financesonline.com/number-of-gamers-worldwide/.

Baker, L. (2019). Therapy in the digital age. In Stone, J. (Ed.), *Integrating technology into modern therapies* (pp. 37–47). Routledge.

Bailenson, J. (2018). *Experience on demand*. W.W. Norton & Company.

Beilinson, J. (2014, May 28). Palmer Luckey and the virtual reality resurrection. https://www.popularmechanics.com/technology/gadgets/a12956/palmer-luckey-and-the-virtual-reality-resurrection-16834760/.

Bell, L. (2017, June). *Qwake Tech's AR helmet helps firefighters see through smoke and get out of fire five times faster*. https://www.forbes.com/sites/leebelltech/2017/06/30/qwake-techs-ar-helmet-helps-firefighters-see-through-smoke-and-get-out-of-fire-five-times-faster/#eecd0e71f664.

Bellani, M., Fornasari, L., Chittaro, L., & Brambilla, P. (2011). Virtual reality in autism: State of the art. *Epidemiology and Psychiatric Sciences*, 20(3), 235–238.

Bricken, M., & Byrne, C. M. (1993). Summer students in virtual reality: A pilot study on educational applications of virtual reality technology. In A. Wexelblat (Ed.), *Virtual reality applications and explorations*. Academic Press Professional.

Brooks, F. P., Jr. (1999, November/December). *What's real about virtual reality?* Computer Graphics and Applications Special Report. http://www.cs.unc.edu/%7Ebrooks/WhatsReal.pdf.

Burns-Nader, S. (2019). Technological tools for supporting pediatric patients through procedures. In Stone, J. (Ed.), *Integrating technology into modern therapies* (pp. 181–193). Routledge.

Clarke, M. (2019, July). *Some prisons are using virtual reality for reentry and other programs*. https://www.prisonlegalnews.org/news/2019/jul/2/some-prisons-are-using-virtual-reality-reentry-and-other-programs/.

Deemer, A., Swenor, B, Fujiwara, K., Deermeik, J., Ross, N., Natale, D., Bradley, C., Werblin, F., & Massof, R. (2019). Preliminary evaluation of two digital image processing strategies for head-mounted magnification for low vision patients. *Translational Vision Science and Technology 8*(1), 1–8.

Dudley, D. (2018, December). Virtual reality used to combat isolation and improve health. *AARP Magazine.* https://www.aarp.org/home-family/personal-technology/info-2018/vr-explained.html.

Ellis, C., (2018, September). *Are VR simulators in the future of pilot training?* https://www.aircharterservice.com/about-us/news-features/blog/are-vr-flight-simulators-the-future-of-pilot-training.

Irvine, K. (2017). *XR: VR, AR, MR—What's the difference?* https://www.viget.com/articles/xr-vr-ar-mr-whats-the-difference/.

Jin, W., Birckhead, B., Perez, B., & Hoffe, S. (2017). Augmented and virtual reality: Exploring a future role in radiation oncology education and training. *Applied Radiation Oncology*, pp. 13–20. https://www.researchgate.net/publication/327228829.

Lamb, R., & Etopio, E. (2019). VR has it. In Stone, J. (Ed.), *Integrating technology into modern therapies* (pp. 80–93). Routledge.

Mandal, S. (2013). Brief introduction of virtual reality & its challenges. *International Journal of Scientific & Engineering Research, 4*(4), 304–309. https://www.ijser.org/researchpaper/Brief-Introduction-of-Virtual-Reality-its-Challenges.pdf.

Maples-Keller, J. L., Bunnell, B. E., Kim, S. J., & Rothbaum, B. O. (2017). The use of virtual reality technology in the treatment of anxiety and other psychiatric disorders. *Harvard Review of Psychiatry, 25*(3), 103–113.

Milijic, M. (2019, October 15). 29 virtual reality statistics to know in 2020. Leftronic. Retrieved from https://leftronic.com/virtual-reality-statistics/?fbclid=IwAR3eUCC-3u8eWvgMAEzMhijoJoEjLK3SbBnXVHqeb2cIV3I8iAVbXiDJJ9c.

Prensky, M. (2001). Digital natives digital immigrants. *On the horizon (MCB University Press) 9*(5), 1–6. https://www.marcprensky.com/writing/Prensky%20-%20Digital%20Natives,%20Digital%20Immigrants%20-%20Part1.pdf.

Presnall, B. (2019). *International military cooperation with medical VR training.* https://www.researchgate.net/publication/334733435_International_military_cooperation_with_medical_VR_training_International_military_cooperation_with_medical_VR_training.

Rizzo, A., & Shilling, R. (2017). Clinical virtual reality tools to advance the prevention, assessment, and treatment of PTSD. *European Journal of Psychotraumatology, 8*(5), 1–21.

Rubin, P. (2014). *The inside story of Oculus Rift and how virtual reality became reality.* https://www.wired.com/2014/05/oculus-rift-4/.

Szoldra, P. (2018, October). *The Airforce used VR to train pilots in half the time at a fraction of the cost.* https://taskandpurpose.com/air-force-vr-pilot-training.

Stone, A. (2017, July). *How virtual reality is changing military training.* https://insights.samsung.com/2017/07/13/how-virtual-reality-is-changing-military-training/.

Stone, J. (2016). Board game play therapy. In O'Connor, K., Schaefer, C. & Braverman, L. (Eds.), *The handbook of play therapy, second edition.* (pp. 309–323). Wiley.

Stone, J. (2019). Digital games. In Stone, J. & Schaefer, C. (Eds.), *Game play (3ʳᵈed.).* Wiley.

Stone, J. (2020). *Digital play therapy: A clinician's guide to comfort and competence.* Routledge.

Wilson, C. J., & Soranzo, A. (2015). The use of virtual reality in psychology: A case study in visual perception. *Computational and Mathematical Methods in Medicine.* https://www.ncbi.nlm.nih.gov/pmc/articles/PMC4538594/pdf/CMMM2015-151702.pdf.

9

MOBILE GAMING

Frans Mäyrä and Kati Alha

This chapter will briefly outline the success story of mobile games, along with the associated developments in the culture of mobile gaming, and will highlight several of the relevant debates and research trends of this quickly developing field. The focus is on three major turns or periods of mobile gaming: the early history of handheld gaming devices and cell phones; the smartphone era and the birth of the contemporary mobile gaming ecosystem; and, finally, the emergence of location-based and mixed reality mobile gaming. The chapter discusses the multiple, distinctive features and consequences of these different varieties of mobile gaming, for the actual gaming content, game development, and industry practices as well as for the people who play games, and for the culture and society that is immersed in gaming.

Introduction

While computer and console video games used to be the defining forms for digital gaming, mobile games have arguably established themselves as the contemporary, dominant sites for digital play. This development has taken place rather quickly over a timespan of only a couple of decades, and transformation has impacted on both the contents and practices of gaming as well as the associated gaming technologies and business models. Simultaneously, the detachment of digital play from fixed locations in homes and dedicated video gaming arcades has spread games and play into everyday lives in an unprecedented manner. The pervasive character and ease of access of mobile gaming is connected with several social and cultural changes: suddenly, almost everyone seems to own a gaming-capable device, and while there has been a celebration of mobile gaming helping games to "go mainstream," there have also been concerns (by gamers and non-gamers alike) that the associated changes have not all been for the good.

This chapter will briefly outline the success story of mobile games, describe the associated developments in the culture of mobile gaming, and highlight several of the relevant debates and research trends of this quickly developing field. We will particularly focus on three major turns or periods of mobile gaming: the early history of handheld gaming devices and cell phones; the smartphone era and the birth of the contemporary mobile gaming ecosystem; and, finally, the emergence of location-based and mixed reality mobile gaming. We shall discuss the multiple, distinctive features and consequences of these different varieties of mobile gaming, for the actual gaming content, game development, and industry practices as well as for the people who play games and for the culture and society that is immersed in gaming.

From the Margins into the Mainstream: The Rise of Mobile Gaming

The evolution of mobile communications has been a relatively fast process and has led to deep social and cultural transformations. According to the data gathered and published by the UN's International Telecommunications Union (ITU, 2019), at the end of 2018 there were already more mobile phones than people on the planet. While over a billion people still lived without access to electricity (not to mention more fundamental issues such as clean water, for example), there were over eight billion active mobile cellular connections around the world while global human population numbers still fell below the eight billion mark in late 2018 (Murphy, 2019).

Our studies of game playing in Finland show that in less than a decade (2009–2018), the share of people playing games with mobile devices has risen rapidly from 44% to 57%. Also, all of the other devices and platforms that are used for playing games (such as personal computers, video gaming consoles, or playing games on web services such as Facebook) were clearly less popular compared to mobile gaming (Karvinen & Mäyrä, 2009; Kinnunen, Lilja, & Mäyrä, 2018).

While such figures are interesting indications of the changing direction of practices and behaviors, the underlying reasons, and also the consequences for game players, gaming content and the society at large are rather complex. Much of the emerging change is rooted in fast developments in the underlying information and communication technologies and in the manufacture of consumer electronics. The first handheld "mobile phone" that was demonstrated by Motorola in 1971 weighted two kilograms and was a completely different kind of device than the slim and powerful touchscreen smartphones of today. While this technological evolution took place, the understanding of what a "mobile game" was or could be was also radically changing. Thus, there are several important phases in this history that are useful to review in this context, at least in outline.

Early History and Development of Mobile Games

As a starting point, it is not particularly self-evident what a *mobile game* is. Despite there being a long history of play and games, many (if not most) games are not fixed to a particular place. For example, it is easy to carry a deck of cards and start a spontaneous session of solitaire pretty much anywhere, any time. Evidence even exists of specific "traveler sets" of dice and board games being used two thousand years ago by the Roman emperor Claudius (10 BCE–AD 54; see Joannou, 2007). For many uses, carrying compact playing pieces such as suitable bones or stones might have been something preferred by, for example, early traveling hunters and gatherers. Mobile gaming has other early roots in various travel practices and early forms of media and technology that have been discussed in research (see, e.g., Farman, 2011; Mattern, 2017). Adopting a media archaeology approach, Jussi Parikka and Jaakko Suominen (2006) have discussed the changes in mobility practices and mechanical consumer entertainment that have laid the foundation for many modern cultural forms, mobile gaming included, particularly during the 19th century.

Most directly, it is possible to see contemporary mobile games emerging specifically from at least two precursors: first, from the long history of physical toys, cards, and other playing pieces and, second, from early computer and video games. The miniaturization of electronics has proceeded rapidly, and already in the late 1970s the first generation of simple, handheld electronic games were being made commercially available. Examples of these early games included Mattel Auto Race (1976) and Merlin (1978). Probably the most popular line of products in the evolution of single-purpose, mobile electronic gaming devices was the *Game & Watch* product series originally manufactured by Nintendo between 1980 and 1991. Computer and video gaming and their underlying technologies continued to evolve, even into extensive virtual game worlds, yet it was the earliest video game generations that demonstrated the simple and clear formulas of game design that have remained influential for mobile gaming for decades.

Many of the early entries into mobile gaming were basically attempts to re-produce some of the successful earlier arcade video games in a form suitable for small-scale electronics. Not much original innovation in terms of actual gaming content was going on at this stage, with the exception of Nintendo; these were primarily consumer electronics manufacturers attempting to emulate video games, rather than companies with game design know-how of their own. One example of this is how Nokia (a Finnish company that became a leading mobile phone manufacturer in the 1990s and early 2000s) implemented Snake (1997) into its handsets (More, 2009). *Snake* was used to pilot some technologies that only later became popular, such as an infrared link functionality that allowed player-versus-player action. However, as for most of the early mobile phone games, the typical use of *Snake* was for single-player gaming (Kuorikoski, 2015).

As internet and online gaming started to grow in popularity, there were many expectations directed toward mobile internet and gaming. The first industrial standard for mobile internet was called Wireless Application Protocol (WAP) and was released with much hype and marketing in 1999. Compared to the visually striking and technically advanced forms that computer and console video games of the era were reaching, mobile gaming in the late 1990s could provide only rather modest offerings. A typical WAP game was a slow-paced black-and-white experience on a small screen. These games could basically just display text or small static graphics screens, and each player action was followed by a rather lengthy waiting period as the next screen slowly downloaded from the server over the cellular connection. However, the future potential surrounding the field was already being seen at the time. The mobile handset manufacturer Nokia is again a good example of this as it invested heavily into mobile gaming, and even launched a dedicated "N-Gage" series of gaming phones (2003; 2004). To circumvent the limitations of slow downloads, games for N-Gage phones were distributed in a gaming-cartridge style in memory cards that were packaged in video game styled boxes.

The evolution of mobile gaming took divergent directions from the start. Christian McCrea (2011) has discussed two related and parallel developments distinguishing between "mobile" and "portable" games and play. In this concept, while mobile games are focused on delivering a fast and easy means of distraction, portable gaming aims at home console or computer game styled, challenging gameplay with deep involvement and long play-cycles but adapted to small devices.

Smartphone Era: A Revolutionary Turn in Mobile Gaming

In discussions of mobile devices, it is often stated that the iPhone (produced by Apple in 2007) revolutionized the entire mobile communications industry. It is notable that this transformation was not brought about by any single technological breakthrough. All elements of the original iPhone had been available prior to its launch, but the novel user experience provided by the highly simplified, touchscreen-based user interface made the impact of iPhone greater than the sum of its parts. The final key element in the success of the iPhone was introduced in 2008, namely, the App Store. There had been several attempts to establish online stores for sales and the digital distribution of software before Apple's iOS App Store, but when combined with the increasing popularity of iPhone, the mobile "app ecosystem" suddenly exploded. The number of small pieces of mobile phone software – "apps" – available in the built-in iPhone store grew from an initial 500 into the millions that are available today. Concurrently, there were parallel developments, particularly in Google's Android ecosystem (also first introduced in 2008).

With new generations of cellular networks (3G, 4G, 5G), powerful and relatively affordable touchscreen consumer devices, and a constantly updated stream of software and services, the contemporary landscape of mobile gaming now looks very different from that seen at the turn of the century. As a consequence, our understanding of what mobile games are and what they can do has changed accordingly.

The early phases of mobile game design were often focused on the miniaturization and simplification of existing video games, largely due to the limitations of the available computing power, memory, and the restricted user interfaces in small handheld devices. As research and development moved forward, it became more apparent that mobile games could have unique strengths that other gaming platforms could not provide. Our own research group in Tampere, Finland, was taking part in this development in the early 2000s, and it is interesting to reflect on how the early expectations and analyses of the time have come true (or not) during the first two decades of the "mobile era."

While much of the commercial mobile game development energy was driven toward overcoming the multiple technical and business challenges of this emerging industry sector, the early interest of researchers and innovators was on targeting what could be seen as a "truly mobile" game. This was based on the realization that mobile phones are first of all built for communication and maintaining social relations. Furthermore, as the device is intimately connected with the daily lives and movements of individuals, future potentials could lie in various "contextual" gaming applications that take information such as time, place, or situational context into account while offering novel gaming experiences. In our MOGAME research project (2003–2004), we conducted a future-oriented user study, discussing alternative scenarios for the future of mobile gaming in several focus group interview sessions. The potential players featured at the time were particularly concerned about the playability and security of future location-based mobile gaming (Ermi & Mäyrä, 2005). Drawing from such studies and technologies that were available at the time, we were able to design, implement, and test an early location-based mobile multiplayer game in our research project "Songs of the North" (see Lankoski et al., 2004). But it took more than a decade before the use of location information and mixed reality became a mainstream phenomenon, with the launch and exceptional success of Pokémon Go (2016). However, during the intervening years, there were several important developments in the gaming culture that affected the directions that game design and game playing would take.

Mobile Gaming as Casual Gaming

In his book *Casual Revolution*, Jesper Juul (2010, p. 10) writes how game audiences and game designs co-evolve: "The audience learns a new set of conventions, and the next game design can be based on the assumption that the audience knows these conventions, while risking alienating those who do not know them." It can be argued that in recent decades, game culture has simultaneously evolved into multiple and even mutually conflicting directions. While the passionate fans and hobbyists of complex computer and video games have played a part in pushing certain genres into ever more ambitious forms, the developments left large parts of the population behind. In our 2008 survey study, only about 8%

of respondents confessed to being a gamer or game hobbyist, although the majority actually reported playing games – many even quite actively (Kallio et al., 2007). When our survey instruments explicitly mentioned that playing solitaire or lottery games or filling in a crossword puzzle are also considered as game playing, we gained a more comprehensive picture where about 88% of the study population reported playing something at least monthly, and almost everyone confessed to having played something (Kinnunen et al., 2018). Yet, the majority of these people appeared to feel excluded from game culture or at least did not accept being a "gamer" or game hobbyist as being part of their identity.

Mobile phones have had an important role in the transformation and "mainstreaming" of video gaming in society. This change has taken place during the wider developments of casual gaming and play cultures becoming visible elements in late modern culture and society. A parallel development has taken place in social media, where services like Facebook began to reach substantial populations and also to distribute games as one element of the platform, simultaneous with the rise of the modern smartphone. A formative moment for future success took place when the Facebook Platform and API (which makes third-party services on Facebook possible) was released in May 2007. It should also be noted that in Facebook, the first generation of games were derivative – for example, when a Scrabble (1938) clone Scrabulous (2007) became popular. A series of games like *Zombies* and *Vampires* (2007) were designed to utilize social network and game mechanics as a viral distribution and marketing strategy. As the casual gaming style of Facebook games was fine-tuned, more ambitious yet accessible games like Happy Farm (2008) and *FarmVille* (2009) emerged.

It became clear that the game design of casual games was inseparably intertwined with their business models. Advertisements and micropayments became linked with time-based game mechanics that were designed to lock players into loops of visiting and revisiting the game to, e.g., plant and harvest their virtual crops at regular intervals as featured in *FarmVille*. Much of these developments were soon repeated in mobile phone gaming – for better or for worse. For example, the mobile game developer Supercell released in 2012 a mobile "farming game" called *Hay Day* that replicates and further develops much of the design and game mechanics of *FarmVille*, including its freemium business logic.

The research of casual games on Facebook and mobile platforms suggests that they are symptomatic of the wider change in directions that digital game cultures were taking. The immersive and challenging games developed in genres such as adventure, role-playing, and strategy computer games were based on the expectation that a player would be willing and able to dedicate tens or perhaps hundreds of hours to progressing and learning in a game. However, the needs and life situations of many people are different. A preference for simple, ritualistic, and non-immersive games became increasingly clear in the early 2000s, and casual social and mobile games were able to cater for those players. Game playing was not necessary the primary activity for such heterogeneous user groups, and games were played for numerous and also instrumental reasons – for example passing time, for taking their minds off work, or for creating and maintaining personal space (Mäyrä et al., 2017). Related to this, the discourses surrounding gaming changed, and new casual design values emerged in the industry (Kuittinen et al., 2007; Kultima, 2009).

Some studies connect this change to gender-specific play patterns. The argument is that males and females appear to have somewhat different priorities and orientations in gaming. For example, mobile gaming in "bite-sized chunks of time" (around 5–10 minutes) on one's smartphone while commuting has been seen as something that appeals more easily to women than games that are designed for dedicated, multiple-hour long sessions (Cohen, 2009). Female game players also appear to have a preference for casual game genres, and in surveys of large player populations (such as those featured in the Quantic Foundry data that are based on over 270,000 players responses; Yee, 2017), popular game types such as family or farm simulation games, and "match-three" games (e.g., *Bejeweled*, 2001; *Candy Crush Saga*, 2012) mostly have female players – 69% women versus 31% men on average. It should be noted, though, that such socio-culturally mediated gendering of game playing can change as gender representations in the gaming content and gendered or discriminating practices in game fandom and game development change (Anable, 2018; Chess, 2017; Shaw, 2015).

While mobile gaming has undeniably broadened the audience of gaming, it has generally not received similar levels of appreciation and approval as games based on more traditional platforms. As long as mobile games have existed, they have been considered as a less serious or less valuable form of gaming that is suitable to fill gaps in time, before having the time to get into "real games." The casual nature of mobile games has further decreased their status among gamer communities. In gamer discussions, mobile games are devalued as being less "real," which is a problematic development. These attitudes and discussions exclude large sections of audiences and their preferences and effectively function as gatekeepers for new audiences (Consalvo & Paul, 2019). Overall, the devaluation of mobile gaming reflects how male-dominated game culture still is, and how much certain design conventions and complexity are valued, while discrediting games with a lower threshold of entering. Due to the gender division in casual games, the excluded audiences are typically female dominated, further emphasizing the exclusionary and discriminatory dynamics affecting gaming communities.

Freemium Model and Mobile Games: The Changing Ecosystems

The revenue models for mobile games have changed throughout time from pre-installed attractions and selling points of the device itself and pay-per-play SMS message games. While the games and their revenue models have evolved, the significance of their economics has dramatically increased. When mobile games first arrived on smartphones, games typically applied what is called a premium business model that entailed a one-time purchase fee. Due to the saturation of the market, prices quickly came down, making it difficult to sell mobile games for higher prices. The free-to-play model was an answer to this problem. In this model, games are offered free to download and play but show in-game advertisements and offer voluntary in-app purchases during gameplay to generate their income. Players can typically spend money to advance faster, make play easier or more convenient, unlock content, or customize their game world.

Free-to-play games had already proven to be successful in other platforms such as online multiplayer games and social network games. However, bringing the model into mobile platforms (roughly from 2010 onwards) ended up being one of the biggest success stories in the game business. It has also proven to be a crucial factor in how mobile games became as large a phenomenon as they are today. In less than a decade, development escalated to a point where almost all of the top-grossing mobile games had adopted the model. In a somewhat problematic dynamic, most players play these games for free, and among the small minority of paying players, the majority of the revenue is generated from a small number of high spenders. According to one market study, as few as 1.6% of mobile free-to-play game players spend any money on the game (Swrve, 2019), although the distribution is highly dependable on the game. Drawing high profits and being dependent on a small number of high spenders have been criticized as being exploitative, and there are multiple social and psychological techniques these games rely on to drive a small portion of players to become high spenders (Shi et al., 2015; Zagal et al., 2013).

The market for mobile free-to-play games is highly competitive and dominated by companies with the possibility to gain enough players from their existing player base or through paid acquisition such as advertising. While companies such as Supercell and King have stayed at the peak of the top-grossing list for several years, new and smaller companies might not make enough with their games for them to be profitable enough to sustain their business.

As the free-to-play model requires players to make in-app purchases during gameplay, the games must be designed with the model in mind. This means that mobile free-to-play games share many design features. As the revenue is gained during gameplay and not beforehand, typically the games are never-ending, offering constantly more content and updates to keep the players interested and the games profitable. Similarly, as players need to be encouraged to pay for extra content, the games can include intentional hindrances and inconveniences that can be bypassed with money. For instance, *Candy Crush Saga* includes levels that are made more difficult than others, designed to monetize the game and drive players to buy items to pass the levels. In *Pokémon Go*, the inventory sizes are limited, which increases the effort the player needs to use on item management. However, inventories can be enlarged with money or in-game currency.

To prevent a player from advancing through the content too quickly, many mobile free-to-play games include waiting or grinding element in their mechanics. This is connected to monetization as well, as players can pay to skip timers or boring content with money or in-game currency. For instance, *Candy Crush Saga* has an incorporated mechanic of lives, which are consumed when the player fails to pass a level. Lives can be regained by waiting, by paying, or with the help of other playing friends. In *Harry Potter: Wizards Unite* (2019), spell energy is used for most actions in the game. Players can regain the energy by visiting inns by walking or by using in-game currency.

It is important to note that while the top-grossing charts have been conquered by free-to-play games, games with other revenue models still exist on mobile platforms.

Location-Based and Mixed Reality as the Future of Mobile Gaming?

There are several technological advancements that have been incorporated into mobile devices that games have taken advantage of. In addition to the general increase in processing power, these include touch screens, accelerometers, camera inputs, and location tracking.

Location data has been used in mobile games for as long as technology has allowed it, but mostly in research prototypes, indie experimentations, and small commercial games that stayed on the margins of gaming. *Ingress* (2012) from Niantic reached enough commercial success to sustain the game, but it was not until the company released their second game, *Pokémon Go*, that location-based games attained a mainstream status. *Pokémon Go* combined a popular, well-suited brand and a successful marketing campaign and also managed to create significant hype around the upcoming game (Alha et al., 2019; Mäyrä, 2017). The game was easy to approach and included new, exciting playing styles that the broad audience was not yet used to. *Pokémon Go* opened gaming experiences to audiences that had not yet previously played mobile games (Koskinen et al. 2019).

After the success of *Pokémon Go*, other companies produced their own location-based games to gain their share of the increased interest. *Walking Dead: Our World* (Next Games, 2018), *Ghostbusters World* (Next Age, 2018), *Jurassic World Alive* (2018), and *Harry Potter: Wizards Unite* all combine a known brand with gameplay that involves physical movement. None of these games have achieved similar success to *Pokémon Go*, but some have nevertheless reached commercial profitability. The future of mobile gaming will most likely feature even more attempts to bring location-based gaming to big crowds and also to create smaller, location-specific installations.

It is interesting to note that although games such as *Pokémon Go* and *Harry Potter: Wizards Unite* both include artificial reality (AR) features to catch creatures in "real environments," this feature is rarely used. Using the AR feature makes the creature appear and move against surroundings recorded with the smartphone's camera, but because catching is harder and drains the battery faster, most players turn it off (Paavilainen et al., 2017). To achieve more widespread popularity, technology must not be an obstacle for playing the game and must provide real added value to it. The location-based AR game *Minecraft Earth* (2019) tries to tackle this by including the building of Minecraft environments in AR mode and making it possible to join other players to build these cooperatively. Thus, in a wider picture, the direction of location-based gaming has oscillated between artistic, societal, and commercially motivated developments (Leorke, 2019).

Discussion

While high production value "AAA" games on PC and console platforms have evolved as immersive audio-visual and narrative experiences, mobile games tend to offer different kinds of experiences. Technological restrictions due to smaller screens, limited input possibilities, and lower hardware performance all have their effects on the platform, making mobile phones especially suitable for casual games. The casual nature of mobile games is what has made them as successful and helped them reach larger audiences than any other game platform, but within gaming cultures, this has not been seen only as a positive development. Mobile games are often treated as a lesser form of gaming, and one of the reasons for opposition to the rise of mobile gaming is the perceived threat it presents to established forms of gaming. However, the mobility and sensors in smartphones have opened new opportunities, as witnessed by the rise of location-based games. Possibly the most controversial and debated feature of contemporary mobile games is the free-to-play revenue model. Fears of the model ruining game culture have often been voiced (Alha et al., 2014), and the rising ethical issues that have arisen have already provoked efforts to regulate the gaming industry. However, as the model has become more common, it has also started to become normalized, and the revenue model has already become largely accepted as an integral part of certain kinds of games. Furthermore, new generations are embracing mobile devices as an equal gaming environment to other gaming platforms.

Smartphones are ever-present and offer constant distractions for the mind when needed. Mobile gaming sessions require less preparation than most other games and can be played anywhere, anytime. This makes mobile games also susceptible for problematic and excessive use. Nevertheless, according to a meta-study by Panova and Carbonell (2018) on smartphone addiction, it might be more appropriate to talk about problematic use rather than actual addiction in the context of mobile gaming. The constant presence of stimuli and distractions has become problematic to many, and excessive use, impulse control problems, and negative consequences that can harm relationships and work are all present in problematic smartphone use. However, there is not enough evidence to warrant speaking about a widespread mobile gaming addiction in society (Billieux et al., 2015; Panova & Carbonel, 2018). As a counter argument, breaks with mobile gaming can relieve stress (Snodgrass et al., 2014) and thus function as a counterforce to the experiences of a hectic, performance-oriented society.

The rise of casual and mobile gaming can also be considered within the context of changing norms, values and attitudes. Having a smartphone in your pocket is an opportunity for game play to become more pervasive, but people will not play games (at least not as much) if they feel it is powerfully sanctioned against or if their culture and society emphasises contradictory values and behaviour models. The increasing presence and popularity of mobile game play may be an indication of higher emphasis and cultural significance being placed upon play and playfulness in society more generally. One discussion in this area concerns the vision of a "Ludic Society" or an "Era of Games," where play, games, and associated ludic practices would become culturally dominant in a late modern society (see, e.g., Mäyrä, 2017; Zimmerman, 2015).

While children's play has had an accepted place in society at least for the modern period (Aries, 1965), adult play has been much more tightly regulated and controlled. However, there are indications that the relationship between work and leisure is changing, and concurrent with the move from an industrial society to a late modern society, there is also an increasing need for adult creativity and playfulness (Florida, 2004; McRobbie, 2016). In contemporary and future societies, there is also a growing demand for people who can fluently interact with data and information and engage in a creative manner with interactive representations, simulations, and other kinds of dynamic, complex systems. Thus, middle-aged adults on the streets playing *Pokémon Go* and other location-based, augmented, or mixed reality games with people younger (and older) than themselves might be a signal of a broader "ludification" of culture and society, where game playing is a normal, acceptable, or even appreciated element in almost everyone's lives.

Alternative, critical perspectives on the rise of mobile gaming and augmented reality technologies are nevertheless important to take into account. The commercial exploitative monetization strategies that often focus on a small vulnerable minority of users have already cast a shadow on the ethics of the entire mobile gaming industry. Furthermore, if we consider a potential future development where multiple "augmented layers" of gaming realities are imposed on top of our shared social and physical spaces everywhere we go, possibly even with the help of prosthetic technologies such as always-on AR eyeglasses (as the logical next step from our increasingly obsessive patterns of smartphone usage), there is a real danger of increased social fragmentation, a radical loss of privacy, and a manipulation of perceived reality with commercial or political motives. In this line of thinking, mobile gaming of the future could provide novel opportunities for alienation, exploitation, and even oppression.

The historical debate on various video game effects nevertheless suggests that it is typical to overestimate the impact of games on our lives. While the trend toward pervasive and even compulsive use of smartphones is well documented and debated, the few existing studies on this topic suggest that people who could be described as "addicted" to checking their smartphones constantly are more drawn toward the social media updates than mobile gaming (see, e.g., Jeong et al., 2016). However, with all its creative and stimulating potential, mobile gaming remains embedded within this wider, problematic trajectory.

References

Alha, K., Koskinen, E., Paavilainen, J., Hamari, J., & Kinnunen, J. (2014) Free-to-play games: Professionals' perspectives. In Proceedings of Nordic DiGRA 2014.

Alha, K., Koskinen, E., Paavilainen, J., & Hamari, J. (2019). Why do people play location-based augmented reality games: A study on Pokémon Go. *Computers in Human Behavior*, 93, 114–122.

Anable, A. (2018). *Playing with feelings: Video games and affect*. Minneapolis: University of Minnesota Press.

Aries, P. (1965). *Centuries of childhood: A social history of family life*. New York: Vintage.

Billieux, J., Maurage, P., Lopez-Fernandez, O., Kuss, D. J., & Griffiths, M. D. (2015). Can disordered mobile phone use be considered a behavioral addiction? An update on current evidence and a comprehensive model for future research. *Current Addiction Reports* 2(2), 156–162. https://doi.org/10.1007/s40429-015-0054-y

Bejeweled (2001). *PopCap Games* [video games].

Chess, S. (2017). *Ready player two: Women gamers and designed identity*. Minneapolis: University of Minnesota Press.

Candy Crush Saga (2012). *King* [video game].

Cohen, A. M. (2009). Closing the gender gap in online gaming. *The Futurist*, 43(6), 10–11.

Consalvo, M., & Paul, C. A. (2019) *Real games: What's legitimate and what's not in contemporary videogames*. Cambridge, MA: The MIT Press.

Ermi, L., & Mäyrä, F. (2005). Player-centred game design: Experiences in using scenario study to inform mobile game design. *Game Studies*, 5(1). Retrieved from http://www.gamestudies.org/0501/ermi_mayra/

Farman, J. (2011). *Mobile interface theory*. New York: Routledge.

FarmVille (2009). *Zynga* [video game].

Florida, R. L. (2004). *The rise of the creative class: And how it's transforming work, leisure, community and everyday life*. New York, NY: Basic Books.

Happy Farm (2008). *Five Minutes* [video game].

Harry Potter: Wizards Unite (2019). *Niantic* [video game].

ITU. (2019). Statistics. Retrieved 6 September 2019, from International Telecommunications Union website: https://www.itu.int/en/ITU-D/Statistics/Pages/stat/default.aspx

Jeong, S. H., Kim, H., Yum, J. Y., & Hwang, Y. (2016). What type of content are smartphone users addicted to? SNS vs. games. *Computers in Human Behavior*, 54, 10–17. https://doi.org/10.1016/j.chb.2015.07.035

Joannou, J. (2007). Have chess set—will travel. A journey in four parts. Part 1: The early years. *The Chess Collector*, 16(2), 12–18.

Jurassic World Alive (2018). *Ludia* [video game].

Juul, J. (2010). *A casual revolution. Reinventing video games and their players.* Cambridge, MA: The MIT Press.

Kallio, K. P., Kaipainen, K., & Mäyrä, F. (2007). *Gaming nation? Piloting the international study of games cultures in Finland.* Hypermedia Laboratory Net Series 14. Tampere: University of Tampere. Retrieved from http://urn.fi/urn:isbn:978-951-44-7141-4

Karvinen, J., & Mäyrä, F. (2009). *Pelaajabarometri 2009: Pelaaminen Suomessa.* Interaktiivisen median tutkimuksia 3. Tampere: University of Tampere. Retrieved from Tampere University, website: http://urn.fi/urn:isbn:978-951-44-7868-0

Kinnunen, J., Lilja, P., & Mäyrä, F. (2018). *Pelaajabarometri 2018: Monimuotoistuva mobiilipelaaminen.* TRIM Research Reports 28. Tampere: University of Tampere. Retrieved from http://urn.fi/URN:ISBN:978-952-03-0870-4

Koskinen, E., Leorke, D., Alha, K., & Paavilainen, J. (2019). Player experiences in location-based games: Memorable moments with Pokémon GO. In *Augmented reality games I*, (pp. 95–116). Springer.

Kuittinen, J., Kultima, A., Niemelä, J., & Paavilainen, J. (2007). Casual games discussion. *Proceedings of the 2007 Conference on Future Play: Research, Play Share,* 105–112. https://doi.org/10.1145/1328202.1328221.

Kultima, A. (2009). Casual game design values. Proceedings of MindTrek 2009, 58–65. Retrieved from http://portal.acm.org/citation.cfm?doid=1621841.1621854

Kuorikoski, J. (2015). *Finnish video games: A history and catalog.* Jefferson (N.C.): McFarland.

Lankoski, P., Heliö, S., Nummela, J., Lahti, J., Mäyrä, F., & Ermi, L. (2004). A case study in pervasive game design: The Songs of North. Proceedings of the Third Nordic Conference on Human-Computer Interaction, 413–416. Retrieved from https://doi.org/10.1145/1028014.1028083.

Leorke, D. (2019). *Location-based gaming: Play in public space.* New York: Palgrave Macmillan. https://doi.org/10.1007/978-981-13-0683-9

McCrea, C. (2011). We play in public: The nature and context of portable gaming systems. *Convergence,* 17(4), 389–403. https://doi.org/10.1177/1354856511414987

McRobbie, A. (2016). *Be creative: Making a living in the new culture industries.* Cambridge, UK & Malden, MA: Polity.

Mattel Auto Race (1976). *Mattel* [video game].

Mattern, S. (2017). *Code and clay, data and dirt: Five thousand years of urban media.* Minneapolis & London: University of Minnesota Press.

Mäyrä, F. (2017). Pokémon Go: Entering the ludic society. *Mobile Media & Communication,* 5(1), 47–50. https://doi.org/10.1177/2050157916678270

Mäyrä, F., Stenros, J., Paavilainen, J., & Kultima, A. (2017). From social play to social games and back: The emergence and development of social network games. In R. Kowert & T. Quandt (Eds.), *New perspectives on the social aspects of digital gaming: Multiplayer 2* (pp. 11–31). New York: Routledge.

1978 Merlin (1978). *Parker Brothers* [video game].

Minecraft Earth (2019). *Mojang* [video game].

More, J. (2009, January 20). History of Nokia part 2: *Snake* | Nokia Conversations – The official Nokia Blog. Retrieved 16 September 2019, from [archived] Conversations.nokia.com website: https://web.archive.org/web/20110723064106/http://conversations.nokia.com/2009/01/20/history-of-nokia-part-2-snake/

Murphy, M. (2019, April 30). Cellphones now outnumber the world's population. Quartz.com. Retrieved 6 September 2019, from Quartz website: https://qz.com/1608103/there-are-now-more-cellphones-than-people-in-the-world/

Paavilainen, J., Korhonen, H., Alha, K., Stenros, J., Koskinen, E., & Mayra, F. (2017). The Pokémon Go experience: A location-based augmented reality mobile game goes mainstream. In Proceedings of the 2017 CHI Conference on Human Factors in Computing Systems (CHI'17). ACM, New York, NY, USA, 2493–2498. DOI: https://doi.org/10.1145/3025453.3025871

Panova, T., & Carbonel, X. (2018). Is smartphone addiction really an addiction? *Journal of Behavioral Addictions*, 7(2), 252–259. DOI: 10.1556/2006.7.2018.49.

Parikka, J., & Suominen, J. (2006). Victorian snakes? Towards a cultural history of mobile games and the experience of movement. *Game Studies*, 6 (1). Retrieved from http://gamestudies.org/0601/articles/parikka_suominen

Pokémon Go (2016). *Niantic* [video game].

Scrabble (1938) Brunot [board game].

Scrabulous (2007). *Lexulous* [video game].

Shaw, A. (2015). *Gaming at the edge: Sexuality and gender at the margins of gamer culture.* Minneapolis: University of Minnesota Press.

Shi, S. W., Xia, M., & Huang, Y. (2015). From minnows to whales: An empirical study of purchase behavior in freemium social games. *International Journal of Electronic Commerce*, 20(2), 177–207. https://doi.org/10.1080/10864415.2016.1087820

Snake (1997). *Nokia* [video game].

Snodgrass, J. G., Lacy, M. G., Dengah, H. J. F., Eisenhauer, S., Batchelder, G., & Cookson, R. J. (2014). A vacation from your mind: Problematic online gaming is a stress response. *Computers in Human Behavior, 38*(September), 248–260. https://doi.org/10.1016/j.chb.2014.06.004

Swrve. (2019). Swrve 2019 Monetization Report. Retrieved from https://blog.swrve.com/its-here-the-swrve-monetization-report-2019

Yee, N. (2017, January 19). Beyond 50/50: Breaking down the percentage of female gamers by genre. Quantic Foundry website: https://quanticfoundry.com/2017/01/19/female-gamers-by-genre/

Zagal, J. P., Björk, S., & Lewis, C. (2013). Dark patterns in the design of games. Presented at the Foundations of Digital Games 2013. Retrieved from http://www.fdg2013.org/program/papers/paper06_zagal_etal.pdf

Zimmerman, E. (2015). Manifesto for a ludic century. In S. P. Walz & S. Deterding (Eds.), *The Gameful world: approaches, issues, applications* (pp. 19–22). Cambridge, MA: The MIT Press.

Zombies and Vampires (2007). *Commagere & Olson* [video game].

10

THE VIDEO GAME DEBATE

Where Do We Go from Here?

Thorsten Quandt and Rachel Kowert

The debate on video games has evolved considerably in recent years. Previously, the public discussion was dominated by a handful of (often negative) narratives about gaming. In particular, research on aggression, addiction, and other harmful effects played a pivotal role, often just to reinforce already firmly entrenched positions. However, as this volume has shown, innovative and exciting new research directions broaden both the scientific perspective and the public debate and are changing the way how we think and talk about games. Naturally, both well-known and potential new risks need to be discussed but also the many opportunities that arise from games as tools for health improvement, learning and deeper insight into social issues, social exchange, or just having fun with a fascinating pastime. In this concluding chapter, we will therefore briefly recap the findings from this book and on that basis discuss potential future developments for the ongoing *Video Game Debate*.

The Past: Negative Narratives and the Deer in Headlights

The debate on video games has always been multi-layered and complex: in public and the media, gaming has been framed in very specific ways to fit a limited number of narratives. As noted in our introductory chapter, there has been a focus on potential risks, and research on addiction, violence, and harmful effects was quite dominant in the coverage. Video games were, again and again, linked to mass shootings, suicide, and forms of harassment in media coverage, painting a dark and threatening picture of the pastime – a coverage that was plausibly intended for a mostly older audience with no personal experience in gaming. This was contradicting the personal experience of a fun diversion by a younger generation, often leading to a conflict between pro- and anti-gaming groups (which was indeed even fueled by some "public experts" that propelled their media presence and career through sensationalist warnings of extreme effects and feeding a "moral panic"; see Bowman, 2016).

The scientific discussion has always been broader but not without its issues as well: multiple divisions and camps of what may be considered a "discipline" by some but a "field" or even just a topic of disciplinary sub-fields for others led to sometimes fruitful but often paralyzing or even destructive struggles. *Grosso modo,* there was a "methodological divide in game (sic!) research" (Williams, 2005, p. 1), with social scientific research interested in effects on the one side and a humanities tradition aiming at uncovering meaning and context of games on the other. Within these research "families," there were again deep trenches: the humanist tradition was split between narrativists who considered games to be a form of storytelling and ludologists who considered games to be an independent form, primarily focusing on their mechanics (Pearce, 2005). The social-scientific side had its own schism between supporters of strong and negative effects on the one side (Anderson et al., 2010) and researchers who perceived the negative effects as being moderate at best or even nonexistent (Ferguson, 2007) on the other. These internal debates may have been helpful in the self-definition and self-reflection of games research as a nascent field or discipline (see Quandt et al., 2015) and, as such, may be considered to be necessary – but in many ways, they also hindered the further development of games research in other directions. For years, research was somewhat acting like the deer in headlights, staring into the blinding light of these debates instead of moving on.

The Present: Emergence of a (Critical) Multi-Perspective

In recent years, the situation has changed considerably: the public depiction of games is a more differentiated one, with alternative narratives becoming more present, like "games and sports," "health benefits of exergaming," and "games as an economic factor in the entertainment industry," to name but a few. This is also due to the fact that not only society has adapted to games becoming part of mainstream entertainment but also an ongoing evolution of gaming itself, with new genres, playing modes, access and distribution channels, and technological innovations (like virtual reality and augmented reality) changing the way we play games and think about them.

Naturally, this is also reflected in the scientific debate, which indeed seems to have moved on beyond paralyzing struggles between academic "camps" and the focus on just a handful of "traditional" issues that have dominated the debate on gaming for so long. The broadening of research is partially due to several reasons, such as stronger institutional support of games research, which has found its home in specialized associations [like Digital Games Research Association (DiGRA)] and various groups within disciplinary associations [like ACM, ICA, European Communication Research and Education Association(ECREA)] and a new generation of scholars asking different questions and pushing the boundaries of research (based on an already established foundation). It is also partially due to the development of gaming and society, which results in new questions and also demands for research.

This doesn't necessarily mean that the "classic" research interests on the effects of gaming have disappeared from the debate but have evolved and adapted to the changes in gaming itself. Some of this is due to core issues being either settled or normatively set, for example by the World Health Ogranization's decision to include gaming disorder in the International Classification of Diseases 11 (ICD11). The latter wasn't greeted with uniform support, and indeed there have been very critical voices (see, for example, Aarseth et al., 2017) strongly opposing such a move as premature, but in effect, this set a normative reference point for future research (even if one is not in support of it). However, as we can see some various articles in this volume, it did not end the debate on addictive effects of gaming.

In particular, Mark Griffiths' overview of loot boxes in video gaming reveals that new mechanics in gaming may alter their characteristics and the way how they should be understood and categorized, particularly in relation to problem behavior. Indeed, as the author convincingly argues, there is consistent proof that there are links between gambling and loot boxes, and he proposes to at least consider "loot box buying … within a regulatory gambling framework" (Griffiths, 2020, in this volume, p. 16). It is important to note the cautious wording of Griffiths, as the inclusion of chance elements alone is not the main problem here – as these are present as a core mechanic in many games, not only digital ones – but the link to (micro) payments and trading platforms. The question on how to address such issues may be answered with tighter regulation, but some of the problems may also be solved by gamers themselves, as the reliance on loot boxes as a central element of a game and as a way to gain in-game advantages over other players is regarded as bad design and no "fun" by many. For example, the initial massive presence of a paid loot box system in the blockbuster game *Star Wars Battlefront II* (Electronic Arts) lead to a controversy among the fanbase and even a boycott, forcing the publisher to react to the criticism and change said system. Similar reactions of users to unfair and disturbing practices lead to some adaption by the industry, even without the need of regulation. Still, a critical observation of such practices both by academia and regulators may be necessary if the "power of the fans" is not sufficient to push change for the better.

The criticism of the addiction-like qualities of some games is not the only "classic" problem issue in the debate on gaming. Another major other criticism is based on the assumption that users of violent games, and first person shooters in particular, may learn such behavior from the games and/or become more aggressive by some form of (cognitive or emotional) transfer. However, if games can be an effective learning tool, it may be argued that they can also be used for beneficial purposes and, indeed, for individual and societal change for the better. Ruud Jacobs, in his debate on "serious games," argues further, countering such an argument but with a twist: he notes a misleading and false equivalence in the debate on learning effects, as "violent games are not intended to make their players violent, while serious games are purpose-built to change players" (Jacobs, 2020, in this volume, p. 23). That is, the learning effects depend on the intent of the designers and the motivations, use, and perception of the audience as well. As Jacobs puts it: "A mature medium is considered neither a magic bullet nor trivially inert" (ibid.).

The importance of the users, their characteristics, environment, and behavior becomes evident from such discussions. However, especially in effects-oriented games research, the audience of games (beyond being an endpoint of effects, a "recipient") has been strangely absent from the debate as the effects have been historically assumed as uniform and comparable across users (which is in line with a specific psychologist view of all users and their brains reacting the same way to a given stimulus under controlled conditions; see, for a critical debate, Henrich, Heine, & Norenzayan, 2010). In some ways, this type of effects-oriented games research can be regarded to be a revenant of previous media related research traditions and partially being ignorant of the shortcomings and issues with such a view that were already discussed decades ago. Indeed, already at the end of the 1950s, the scientific debate in media and communication research was turning its interest away from a simplifying "what do the media do to people" to the more complex question "what do people do with media." (Katz, 1959, p. 2).

It is reassuring to see that multiple articles in the current issue put the user at the core of their interest, differentiating forms of use, gamer experiences, their characteristics, and even broader aspects of gamer cultures. Such a discussion is necessary – especially as the research shows that in contrast to above-mentioned reductionist view, not all users are equal, nor are they treated as being equal. On the contrary, as Thomas Apperley and Kishonna Gray discuss in their chapter, a stereotypical idea of the "gamer" as a white (underage) male has systematically discriminated other groups within gaming culture or even excluded them from participation. Marginalization may happen along various characteristics of a person, but in particular, gender as well as ethnicity, race, or nationality are major causes for discrimination. While games research hasn't fully ignored these issues, and indeed has intensified research efforts on discrimination and harassment in gaming, the importance of this calls for further research. As Apperley and Gray (2020) note: "Digital play and digital games … must … be understood as technologies that can cultivate and produce equal opportunities just as much as they can embed discriminatory practices." (in this volume, p. 50).

In the following chapter, Ashley Brown and Lis Moberly underline this with their examination of *Twitch*. The most prominent videogame streaming service both offers positive options for participating in a vivid and evolving community but also multiple negative sides, including discrimination as outlined in the previous chapter by Apperley and Gray and multiple economic disparities. Brown and Moberly (2020) conclude that "streaming is a microscope for other active debates surrounding tech" (in this volume, p. 62), and certainly, the issues plaguing *Twitch* are not necessarily limited to this specific platform or streaming as a whole. Comparable problems of discrimination and disparities are recurring in gaming, and they have been known for a while now, arguably without a satisfying response by gamers, the industry, and academia as of yet. The Gamergate controversy and discussions about toxicity pushed some of these issues to the forefront of debate, but many aspects of discrimination and harassment in gaming are still not fully addressed in the debate, and concrete solutions are scarce.

The subsequent chapter by Stephanie Orme picks up this argument in her analysis of esports as an industry, highlighting both the evolution and successes of esports in recent years as it has taken giant developmental leaps to become a multi-billion dollar business. Accordingly, the academic debate has to adapt to such rapid changes – earlier works were (too) preoccupied with the very basic question whether esports is "just" highly competitive gaming or "real" sports, which is probably a moot point as the field has progressed beyond the initial stages of self-reflection. Many "practitioners" of esports do not care about these comparisons with traditional sports – and related analogy questions – any more as they have accepted it (and perform it) as its own form. And indeed, given the evolution toward a massive industry, other questions come into focus, tied to challenges like "regulating esports gambling and managing players' health and well-being" (in this volume, p. 76), as Orme (2020) puts it.

Well-being and health are also at the core of two other articles – one by Anthony Bean on therapeutic uses of video games and one by Jessica Stone on virtual reality (VR), augmented reality (AR), and mixed reality (MR) in mental health treatment. Bean, again, refers to the turn of video games research toward use (from merely effects-oriented approaches) and sketches the notable potential of games for therapeutic interventions by giving numerous concrete examples on how to apply specific games in such a context. An understanding of gaming as a meaningful and emotional experience (with all its pros and cons), and not just as a potential "threat" to minors, broadens the horizon for games research and leads to the insight that some of the inherent logics and goals of games may be beneficial for their users, and particularly so for patients: "Playing video games has the ability to help conquer our own fears by defeating the monsters within the video game" (Bean, 2020, in this volume, p. 592). Jessica Stone in her discussion of extended reality (XR) – comprising AR, VR, and MR – shows further use cases of these technological advancements for therapy. The innovations under the XR umbrella alter the way how we play and perceive games, and they also open up new possibilities for therapy that are not even possible in a "real-life" setting. Transporting patients into environments of choice, giving them specific abilities or characteristics in such an environment, confronting them with virtual objects and actors, training specific situations, all in an easy to control and manipulate setting, are just some of the benefits. Many of these are true for non-XR games as well, but deep "immersion" and the feeling of "presence" clearly make a difference – especially in therapy. Again, the uses are abundant, as Stone (2020) concludes: "Personal development, coping and interpersonal skills, catharsis, abreaction, and much more, through the use of XR, can be explored, identified, practiced, and integrated into day-to-day life" (in this volume, p. 105).

Besides XR, another technological advancement was missing from the previous volume of the *Video Game Debate* – mobile gaming. In recent years, this has arguably overtaken more traditional forms of "desktop" or "living room" gaming and has become ubiquitous. Mäyrä and Alha (2020) briefly sketch the development of multiple forms of mobile gaming and then discuss the features and consequences of these. Through smart phones and other mobile devices, gaming is indeed enjoyed anywhere, any time these days, and according to the authors, we are living in a "culture and society that is immersed in gaming" (in this volume, p. 107). Although, despite the omnipresence of gaming, one should not be either over-enthusiastic or despair in face of the potential threats, as this would just repeat issues that plagued the earlier academic debate on video games with a polarization of viewpoints in the expectation of massive effects on individual and society. Or, as Mäyrä and Alha (2020) phrase it, "The historical debate on various video game effects nevertheless suggests that it is typical to overestimate the impact of games on our lives" (in this volume, p. 118).

In this sense, it's crucial for the academic debate to learn from past mistakes and to somewhat "normalize" in its approach and debates. Gaming has matured into an accepted form of mainstream entertainment, with growth and consolidation in the industry; a professionalization of gaming itself (for example in the form of esports); and a growing (sub)differentiation of genres, user groups, and gaming cultures, and research has to adapt this not only in terms of its "objects," but also in terms of approaches and concepts. Indeed, a call for new and broader perspectives beyond a simplistic black-and-white view of gaming concluded the last volume, which already introduced numerous alternative approaches beyond the "traditional" perspective on gaming (as discussed in our introductory chapter to the current volume). The brief overview of the latest additions to the *Video Game Debate* in this volume documents that research has further responded in various ways and that today there are multiple perspectives on gaming productively co-existing. Also, while some of the authors clearly mark the challenges and issues of the latest developments in the field, they also cover the many positive uses of gaming and games-related technological developments (like XR), often in parallel. This is an encouraging development for a research field that has frequently been witness to fierce battles between various pro/con gaming camps and dividing trenches that seemed to be insurmountable. Current games research, it seems, can be critical without being destructive, both toward its object of research, and the academic "other"! This is certainly sign of the anticipated normalization, and an important step for the future of open, fair, and differentiated games research.

The Future: A Cloudy Crystal Ball

As discussed above, the current *Video Game Debate* is both broader and deeper than it was in the past. The developments in the field in concurrence with the differentiation of the academic approaches have propelled the emergence of the current multi-perspective on video gaming. The traditional "issues and risks" oriented approaches to gaming (in particular, discussing addiction and violent content) did not disappear from the picture, but there are more voices to the debate and many more research findings to build upon. In addition to these "classics," new questions and topics have co-evolved with technological advances, new genres, many more user groups, a further consolidation of gaming as an industry, and a growing societal acceptance.

Naturally, such a growing variety is welcome, but it makes predictions on what to expect from the future even more difficult. Scientists have failed miserably in the past when forecasting technological and societal developments, even in a relatively short term. And, indeed, some of the expectations and extrapolations from the last volume of the *Video Game Debate*, which is just a few years old, may look ridiculously outdated in hindsight – either because the predicted future developments happened faster, slower, or not at all. Keeping this warning in mind, we will therefore refrain from looking too deep into what is essentially a very cloudy crystal ball.

Will we see a further diffusion of XR technologies into the mainstream of society? Will we see games in conjunction with wearables? Will we see new forms of distribution or monetization? Will gaming reach new groups in society; will it overcome barriers set up by ignorance and discrimination? Will we see new and exciting uses for health and well-being, personal advancement, and training? To be frank – we don't know for sure. Naturally, there are some more and some less likely developments, and for sure, some "risk" topics like "harassment" and "discrimination in gaming," as well as more "beneficial" topics like "serious games" and "health benefits," will keep research busy for years to come.

What seems to be certain, though (and here it is probably not even necessary to look into the crystal ball): the future evolution of gaming will bring both worrying and exciting developments that need to be critically accompanied by scientific research. And thus the *Video Game Debate* will continue.

References

Aarseth, E. et al. (2017). Scholars' open debate paper on the World Health Organization ICD-11 Gaming Disorder proposal. *Journal of Behavioral Addictions*, 6(3), 267–270. doi: 10.1556/2006.5.2016.088.

Anderson, C. A., Shibuya, A., Ihori, N., Swing, E. L., Bushman, B. J., Sakamoto, A., Rothstein, H. R., & Saleem, M. (2010). Violent video game effects on aggression, empathy, and prosocial behavior in eastern and western countries: A meta-analytic review. *Psychological Bulletin*, 136(2), 151–173. doi: 10.1037/a0018251.

Apperley, T., & Gray, K. (2020). Digital divides and structural inequalities: Exploring the technomasculine culture of gaming. In R. Kowert & K. Gray (Eds.), *The video game debate 2*. New York: Routledge.

Bean, A. (2020). Therapeutic use of video games. In R. Kowert & T. Quandt (Eds.), *The video game debate 2*. New York: Routeldge.

Bowman, N. D. (2016). The rise (and refinement) of moral panic. In R. Kowert & T. Quandt (Eds.), *The video game debate: Unravelling the physical, social, and psychological effects of digital games* (pp. 22–38). New York: Routledge/Taylor & Francis Group.

Brown, A. & Moberly, L. (2020). Twitch and participatory cultures. In R. Kowert & T. Quandt (Eds.), *The video game debate 2*. New York: Routledge.

Ferguson, C. J. (2007). The good, the bad and the ugly: A meta-analytic review of positive and negative effects of violent video games. *Psychiatric Quarterly, 78*(4), 309–316. doi: 10.1007/s11126-007-9056-9.

Griffiths, M. (2020). A brief overview of lootboxes. In R. Kowert & T. Quandt (Eds.), *The video game debate 2*. New York: Routledge.

Henrich, J., Heine, S. J., & Norenzayan, A. (2010). The weirdest people in the world? *Behavioral and Brain Sciences, 33*(2-3), 61–83.

Jacobs, R. (2020). Serious games: Play for change. In R. Kowert & T. Quandt (Eds.), *The video game debate 2*. New York: Routledge.

Katz, E. (1959). Mass communication research and the study of culture. *Studies in Public Communication, 2*, 1–6.

Mäyrä, F. & Alha, K. (2020). Mobile gaming. In R. Kowert & T. Quandt (Eds.), *The video game debate 2*. New York: Routledge.

Orme, S. (2020). Playing to win: The global esports industry and key issues. In R. Kowert & T. Quandt (Eds.), *The video game debate 2*. New York: Routledge.

Pearce, C. (2005). Theory wars: An argument against arguments in the so-called ludology/narratology debate. In *Proceedings of DiGRA 2005*. Retrieved from http://www.digra.org/wp-content/uploads/digital-library/06278.03452.pdf.

Quandt, T., van Looy, J., Vogelgesang, J., Consalvo, M., Elson, M., Ivory, J., & Mäyrä, F. (2015). Digital games research: A survey study on an emerging field and its prevalent debates. *Journal of Communication, 65*(6), 975–996. doi: 10.1111/jcom.12182.

Stone, J. (2020). Extended reality therapy: The use of virtual, augmented, and mixed reality in mental health treatment. In R. Kowert & T. Quandt (Eds.), *The video game debate 2*. New York: Routledge.

Williams, D. (2005). Bridging the methodological divide in game research. *Simulation & Gaming, 36*(4), 447–463. doi: 10.1177/1046878105282275.

INDEX

Printed in Great Britain
by Amazon